# *Light in the* DARKNESS *Oracle*

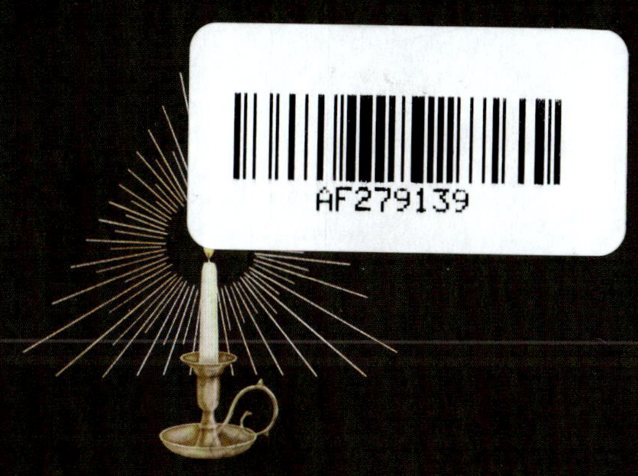

## AN ORACLE OF HOPE & TRANSFORMATION

BY SERENE CONNEELEY

ARTWORK BY CECILIA G.F.

# LIGHT *in the* DARKNESS
## *ORACLE*

AN ORACLE OF HOPE & TRANSFORMATION

Published by Blue Angel Publishing®
10 Trafford Court, Wheelers Hill
Victoria, Australia 3150

*info@blueangelonline.com*
*www.blueangelonline.com*

Edited by Jules Sutherland and Peter Loupelis

Designed by Gemma Christensen

Blue Angel is a registered trademark of Blue Angel Gallery Pty Ltd.

ISBN: 978-1-922574-51-0

Designed in Australia. Printed in China with soy-based inks.

# TABLE *of* CONTENTS

## *Light in the Darkness*



## *Card Messages*

# Welcome, Friend

Come, draw a chair up to the fire and gaze into the dancing orange flames. It's chilly outside, and midnight-dark, but in here, all is cosy and toasty warm. Feel the heat as it paints your cheeks with a radiant, rosy glow. Soak in the comfort of the flickering candlelight as it illuminates what is in your heart — a light so bright it is a beacon for others, and should be a source of strength for you too.

It can be hard to recognise though, since so many of us look outside ourselves for validation. We refuse to imagine ourselves through other people's eyes, instead falling back on our own self-critical summation. And when times seem dark, it can be even harder to see our own worth, our own sparkle, our own light.

But it is there, just waiting for you to acknowledge it, accept it and integrate it, so you can start shining your beautiful light outwards as well as within. In troubled times, it's important to find your own light. To allow challenges to push you forward rather than stay stuck where you are. And to ponder the things you hide, and those you must let go of. Secrets, grief, shame and pain all conceal themselves in the darkness, but you have the power within you to spotlight them with your radiance and force them to the surface for examination, where you can nurture and heal your heart as well as your soul.

Don't worry though that darkness itself is bad, or negative, or against the light. It's not. It's an intrinsic part of the natural world, part of every one and every thing. Both are necessary, and healing, and complement each other. Because as important as it is to shine your light, you must also embrace your shadow, going within to find your own truths and the wisdom you already hold. Focusing only on the so-called light can push you out of balance and into toxic positivity, where problems are minimised, ignored or denied altogether, and a forced cheerfulness and fake smile is pasted over your life, leaving things to fester beneath.

Finding your light doesn't mean pretending that real issues don't exist; rather, it will allow you to see them and put them in perspective, to better deal with them and create real and lasting change. Know that you are not defined by any darkness that has touched your spirit or walked beside you. When you shine a light into the darkness, it will illuminate your strength and hope, revealing your unseen magic so you can integrate and celebrate it. Without darkness, there is no light, no balance, no stars. No wholeness or completion. So embrace every aspect of yourself, be as kind to yourself as you are to others, and activate the joy and wonder that is within you.

I hope this deck will help you find the courage to live the life you dream of, deal with tests and trials, challenge your self-worth so you can accept how brightly you shine, recognise your own light, and look through the darkness to find the stars. There is light and shade in all you feel and all you are. When you can acknowledge this, you'll unlock what's been within you all along, and open your heart to more kindness, empathy, love, magic and wonder.

# Meeting Your Cards

Like you would in any new relationship, take some time to introduce yourself and get to know your deck. Spread the cards out, artwork side up, on a table, your bed, the floor or the earth, and gaze at each image. Do any jump out at you? Which ones do you love best, and are there any you find confronting? It can be fascinating to keep a record of this, then compare how you feel about them after you've worked with them for a while.

Before your first reading, cleanse your deck and imbue the cards with your energy. You might like to:

- Pass the deck through incense smoke.
- Place a large quartz crystal on top of it.
- Leave it out under the full moon to charge for a night.
- Cup the deck between your hands to charge it with your energy.
- Hold it to your heart and pour reiki or another healing energy into it.
- Thumb through the deck, touching each card so it receives your vibration, then shuffle well.

# How to Use Your Deck

There are so many different ways to use an oracle deck, and many different formations. Use your favourite one and do what you're guided to, depending on the situation you're facing and the answers you seek. Or, you might like to experiment with some of the following options.

## *One-Card Readings*

For a simple reading, you can choose a card each morning, and use it as a theme for your day. It might be the card meaning that brings you guidance, it could be the affirmations you'll embrace, or it may be the deities each card features that will help most, as you welcome them in as your patron god or goddess for the day. Or perhaps you'd rather choose a card each night before bed, and let the imagery, words and deity seep into your dreams, providing further insight that way.

You can also choose a card for the week, and repeat one of its affirmations every morning and night, and any other time you need to during the day. Doing this over seven days will reinforce the message of the card, helping your subconscious really start to accept and believe the affirmation and connect with the god or goddess energy.

To select your card, shuffle the deck, thinking either, "What do I need to know today?" or asking a specific question. Then draw a card from the top of the deck, the bottom, or the one you feel most drawn to when they're fanned out. Alternatively, you can work through the cards in order from Card 1 to Card 44, meditating on a new one each day or week, and drawing the energy of that deity and meaning into your subconscious, no matter what your situation. You can also search through the contents list, choose the card that's most relevant to your current issue, and integrate that meaning.

Keep track of your readings, writing them into a journal or typing them up so you can read back through them all later and see patterns emerging — of growth, new understanding, repeated messages and a unique story of fate and meaning that will make sense only to you.

## *Multicard Spreads*

Decide the layout you will use from the below options—or choose your own version—then hold your question in your mind as you shuffle the deck. When you are ready, place your cards in one of the following formations.

# Two-Card Readings

Place one card on the left (Card 1) and one card on the right (Card 2). Consider the meaning of each individual card, then how they work together and influence each other to shed further light on your life in this moment.

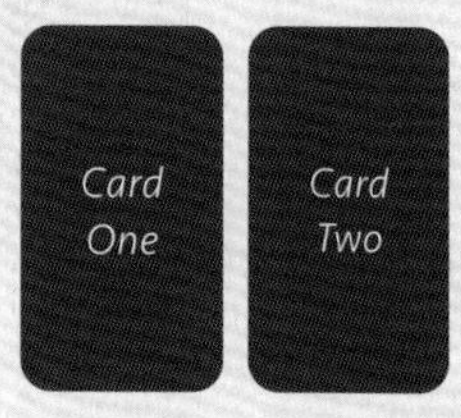


1. What you need to let go of.
2. What you need to bring into your life.

1. What's making you feel stuck.
2. How to move through it and be free of the issue.

1. How you really feel about the situation.
2. What action to take to resolve it.

1. The energy around you right now.
2. How to work with it for the best results.

1. What it is you really want.
2. What you're settling for and need to release.

1. The hidden aspect of the situation you're currently in.
2. The challenge you must overcome to move forward.

1. The aim or goal you're working towards.
2. The thing preventing you from achieving it.

1. Insight into the situation you're facing.
2. Information to help you deal with the problem.

# Three-Card Readings

Place one card on the left (Card 1), one card in the middle (Card 2), and one card on the right (Card 3). Consider the meaning of each individual card and how you feel about them being in the position they're in, then how they influence each other and work together to provide a wider overview. Is there a card you wish wasn't in the spread, or any you wish were? Ponder this as part of the reading.

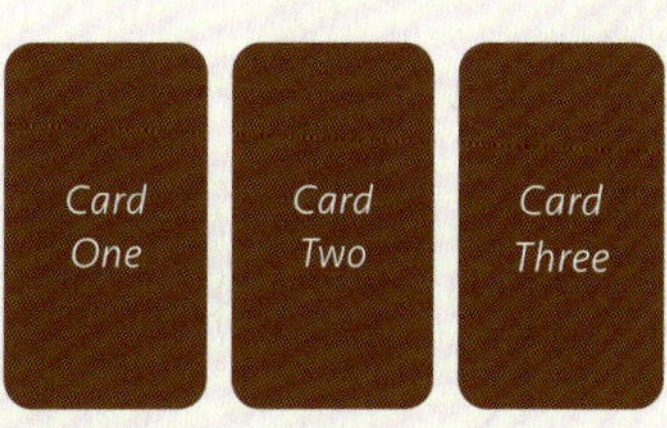


1. What continues to affect you from your past.
2. What is challenging you right now, in the present.
3. What you need to do to resolve the issue you're facing for a brighter future.

1. What is hidden from you and what you need to learn.
2. What you can let go of to improve the situation.
3. What you are doing well and should celebrate.

1. Who you were in the past and the character trait influencing this situation.
2. Who you are now and what you need to do to face it.
3. Who you will become if you continue with things the way they are and don't change course.

# Five-Card Reading

When you have more time, you can extend the past-present-future spread into a longer reading using five cards.

- Start by laying out the first three cards from left to right, with each of the cards giving you insight into the past, present and future, respectively.
- Beneath the row of three, place Card 4 between Card 1 and Card 2 — it bridges the first two cards, past and present, and will reveal more about what led to your current situation.
- Place Card 5 between and below Cards 2 and 3 — it will show what challenge or block you have to deal with to get from the present to the potential future.

# The Year Ahead: A Thirteen-Card Reading

This is a powerful spread to do around New Year's Eve, but since you can start a new year on any day, at any time, you don't have to wait until the end of December to get your overview.

As you shuffle, focus on the next 12 months, then lay out 13 cards — 12 in a circle, with the 13th in the middle. The card in the one o'clock position is for January, the card in the two o'clock position for February and so on, with the centre card representing the theme or overarching challenge for the year ahead.

Alternatively, you might like to place the cards in four rows of three, representing each of the four seasons.

# Speak an Affirmation

Each card message comes with a selection of affirmations
you can work with to reinforce the meaning and lesson
of the card, although of course you can choose your own
if you prefer, or write new ones. Your thoughts are more
powerful than you imagine, and can transform your life for
the better — or the worse. Positive affirmations are potent
reminders to yourself and others about your strengths,
qualities and the intention you want to live with. They can
help you challenge negative views about yourself and stop
self-sabotaging behaviours, influence the way others see
you, and boost your confidence and self-esteem.

Affirmations are like exercises for the mind, making you
stronger and more confident, and reprogramming your
negative thoughts into positive ones, which can, in turn,
change your behaviour. Repeating positive affirmations
before a stressful event has been found to calm your nerves
and increase your confidence, reduce the effects of stress
on the body, and help you better deal with frustration or
anger. If you're stuck in a negative mindset, affirmations
may be the first step out into the light. Rather than talking
yourself into believing you're not good enough—which
most of us do every day—convince yourself that you *are*.
You're ready for this new opportunity. You are strong and
confident. You deserve to achieve what you dream of. You
are loved, and you are enough.

Select the affirmations you want to work with from the
cards you pull—or create your own—and say them out loud

throughout the day, so that you hear your voice speaking positively about yourself. Repeat them regularly, especially first thing in the morning and last thing at night, as well as when you walk to work, travel to see a friend, make meals or hit the gym. Pay attention to how you feel as you say them. Do you struggle to speak the words? Do you feel teary? Do you feel empowered? Do you feel that these statements are not true?

You can also write affirmations out by hand, so you absorb them into your consciousness, then place them somewhere you'll see them throughout the day — on your fridge, a mirror, in your wallet, on a t-shirt. You could program them to pop up as a notification on your phone, or set one printed across an inspiring photo or happy moment as your computer's screensaver. Pull a card each morning and meditate on the positive message, or stare into the mirror and say, "I love you." And mean it.

Just as positive affirmations can reprogram your thinking and increase your confidence, be aware of negative affirmations. They are just as powerful, in a way you *don't* want to harness. "I'm hopeless …", "I'll never get the job …", "I let people walk all over me …", "I'm so stupid, I don't deserve to achieve that goal …" (and so on) will lower your energy, destroy your confidence and dull your enthusiasm — and even worse, can become a self-fulfilling prophecy. People believe what you say, so if you constantly insist that you don't deserve a promotion, your boss will give it to someone else. If you tell everyone you're not good enough, you'll be overlooked for wonderful opportunities. Even worse, *you'll* believe it, and will act as though it's true, not putting yourself forward or even trying to make a dream come true. If you catch yourself trash-talking yourself, override your negative statements with positive self-talk, choosing a positive affirmation that states the opposite of what you were claiming, and thus reinforcing the truth. The more you say it, the more you will believe it, and the more people will see you in a new and better light.

Negative affirmations have great power because they're ingrained and they're usually said with great feeling, but you can neutralise them by taking control of your thoughts, correcting self-critical statements and repeating over and over how happy, healthy and loved you are, until you finally start to believe it and thus make it true. Don't beat yourself up if you continue being negative for a while, though — self-criticism is often a deeply entrenched habit, and it will take some time and awareness to break it. Each time you catch yourself, state, "That is an old thought; I no longer choose to think that way." Or, "I know that's not true; I will stop telling myself that." Then quickly find a positive thought to replace it, and repeat that one.

Also examine any negative statements that feel real to you, and ask yourself seriously if there is any merit to them. Be objective, and argue your case with yourself. Most self-criticism is unfounded, a judging of yourself that is a far harsher standard than you would hold anyone else to. If you look at your statement objectively, you'll usually see it isn't true, in which case, consider why you say it. Are you wanting someone to argue with you and tell you it's not true? Fishing for compliments and validation from others, because you can't give it to yourself? Or does being defeatist now make you feel that you don't have to try to fulfil your dreams? If you're still struggling to untangle all of this, ask a friend for their view, as they're often able to see you more clearly and objectively than you can.

And if your negative statements are true? You have the power to change your behaviour and your attitude, and turn your life around, so do it!

When creating an affirmation, make sure you always word it in the present tense, and in a positive way. "I don't want to be sick anymore" is not an affirmation for good health. Instead state clearly what you *do* want: "I accept perfect health now," or "I am vibrant, healthy and filled with energy." If you want more money, don't affirm your lack but instead assert, "I am prosperous" or "I attract and deserve abundance." The aim is to plant the seeds for present and future prosperity, rather than affirming that you don't have enough in the present, a situation you'll exacerbate by focusing on the negative.

The most effective affirmations will be personal, so if the ones in this deck don't resonate with you, create some with your own wording and style. Affirmations and positive thinking will only get you so far though — you also have to take action. So affirm that you desire and deserve an amazing new job, then start applying for some or learning a new skill so you can transition to the career you crave. Affirm that you are fit and healthy — then take steps to make that true, by moving your body, drinking more water, eating well and staying on top of health checks.

And if you catch yourself being critical of others, let the thought go, then think of a positive quality about that person. Being petty about yourself or anyone else does not become you. It drags you back into the mire of judgement and comparison where no one wins, and reinforces your negativity. Remind yourself that you are filled with light, and with love and hope and magic, and you want to share them with everyone.

## Invoke a Goddess or a God

Each card also has an associated deity you can work with to enhance the situation you're dealing with. Working with the energies of gods and goddesses from around the world can be a powerful tool, as you can invoke their energy and strength to help you with the situation you're dealing with. Calling on the energy of Artemis, the Greek goddess of the moon and the hunt, can help you feel more powerful, determined and capable of facing a challenge. You can invoke Guanyin or Tara, the Buddhist goddesses of compassion, if it's forgiveness, benevolence and peace you require. You can call on Egyptian deities Thoth and Ma'at for issues of justice and balance, or invoke Ceridwen, the Celtic goddess of rebirth, transformation and inspiration, for support in making a change and transforming your life.

Working with these deities can be as simple or elaborate as you wish. The first step is to communicate with them, which for some may be praying, for others a conversation either out loud or as an inner dialogue, while others still will connect through divination, channelling or ritual. You can create an altar devoted to a deity or deities, find a statue or other representation to display, offer sacrifices— of herbs, oils, time, food, crystals or incense—burn a candle in their honour, write them a poem or story, wear a pendant or other jewellery that symbolises them, work with the cycles of the moon or the seasons they're associated with, or dance and sing to exalt them. You might also feel drawn to protect animals in the name of your chosen deity, support a cause they're associated with, or communicate with them through your own art, craft, words or song. You can also research their myths, legends and history, examining the way they've been portrayed throughout time, in stories and song, paintings and sculptures.

Perhaps you'll work with a different deity each day, introduce yourself to a whole pantheon, such as the Celtic, Greek or Egyptian gods, or you may choose to work with one god or goddess exclusively, developing a deep relationship with them, and maybe even choosing to devote yourself to study and be initiated as a priest or priestess of this patron deity. You can start a journal or

Book of Shadows dedicated to one or more of the gods and goddesses you work with, learning more about them, recording their history and the ways they have helped humanity, researching the rites long-ago people performed in their honour, how they are venerated today, and crafting a personal ritual to connect with them.

Pagan gods and goddesses don't need to be worshipped in the same way as in Abrahamic religions — you can speak with them while out in nature, sitting at your altar, in the office or while travelling. To some, working with a deity is like having a friend or partner to confide in, ask advice of, and call on for assistance with healing and protection. To others, these deities are almost like a mother or father, offering comfort and guidance, and still others have a relationship that incorporates more familiar forms of worship. Often you will receive signs they are around you — the Morrigan might send a crow friend, while Bastet directs a cat to cross your path. Others may impart a message through your dreams, coincidences, random snatches of conversations you overhear, or even lines in a magazine article or on TV.

You may prefer to communicate with them through divination. This oracle deck is one such way — as you shuffle the cards, ask for the god or goddess who has a message for you to make themselves known, and work with the card you select. Alternatively, you could consecrate a deck that doesn't include deities as your tool for communication, and know that any reading you do will be from them. You can also try automatic writing and see who turns up, or use a pendulum, runes or scrying to ask them questions.

It doesn't matter whether you believe these deities once existed, still exist, or are more metaphorical than literal. They are powerful archetypes you can draw on and work with to understand yourself better, incorporating their traits into your life and actions, and discovering coping strategies in the lessons they share through their own lives, mysteries and themes. They are archetypes of masculine and feminine, shadow and light, strength and magic, and can help you understand the world, yourself and human nature as you connect with their symbols, work with their energy and invoke their qualities within you.

May you find light in the darkness, and peace in the storms of life.

*Much love, Serene xx*

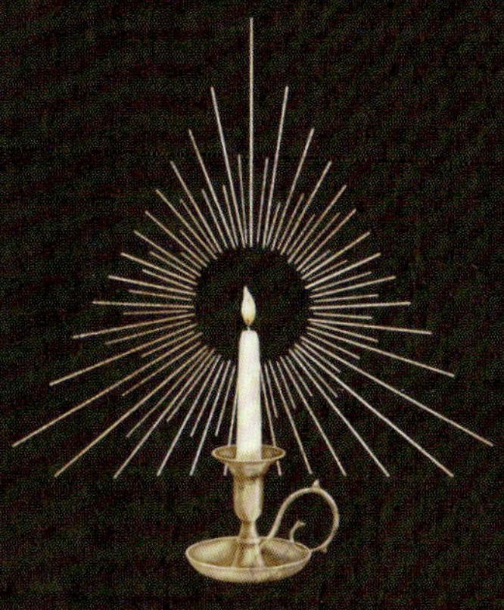

# CARD
## *MESSAGES*

# 1. Be Your Own Guiding Light

*Within your vulnerability are the seeds of great inner strength. Trust yourself. Your current difficulties are forging resilience and power. Embrace both your darkness and your light in order to be your best, most shining self.*

## Message

Sometimes it seems easier to search outside yourself for illumination, not believing you already have the source within, but seek this inner spark. You hold the power to be your own guiding light, no matter how much darkness you feel around you, and you know what is best for you.

Start listening to the stirrings of your heart, the whispers in your mind, and the barely perceptible feelings your body offers up to warn of danger or delight.

Don't worry if you feel a little broken — it doesn't mean you *are* broken, just that you need to rest and recover as a step towards wholeness. Not all destruction is a bad thing. In this situation, it's simply destruction of the thing keeping you from a more fulfilling existence, and transforming your temporarily shattered pieces into a positive force.

Strength is a wonderful trait, but there are times when forcing yourself to continue, no matter how difficult it is, can be unhelpful, even harmful. Sometimes the way forward is in allowing yourself to *not* be strong — to break down, be vulnerable and let others help *you*. In falling apart so you can put yourself back together in a new and better way. Touching the darkness in order to see your own light. Just as moonflowers only bloom at night, some forms of beauty and strength are hewn from the darkness, only able to be seen within its depths, and taking their power and healing from it.

You don't need to shine for others right now. Find your own guiding light and bathe in it yourself, your inner flame rising and illuminating the situation you face. Follow your intuition and inner truths, and blaze with compassion, strength and generosity of spirit. Develop the courage to shine your light so you can find the right path for yourself, and thus discover meaning and new purpose.

Embrace with gratitude those who treat you with kindness and empathy. Clear your life of people and situations that hurt or harm you. Release excess baggage and emotions that no longer serve. And throw off the shackles binding you to the past so you can move forward and awaken to the power and light within you.

## Helpful Deities

Call on Kali, the Hindu goddess of life, death and destruction, and the mother of all. She has unwavering judgement, strong willpower and deep insight, and can help you invoke these traits within yourself. Kali has a reputation as a dangerous, cruel force who wields destruction with joy. But when she lays waste to your dreams, to your patterns, to your life, it's only ever a positive thing — a strategy to push you to take a new and better path, to leave behind the things you no longer need, the things you hold on to out of insecurity and fear. Once the way is clear, you can recreate your life in brilliant new ways and shine your light into the world.

## Affirmations

My light is within me, not outside.

I am not broken; I am becoming who I long to be.

I embrace and integrate my shadow.

I am whole and complete.

I shine my light and dispel the darkness.

2. No Is Not a Bad Word

# 2. No Is Not a Bad Word

*Be considerate of others and help where you can, but not at your own expense. Set boundaries when necessary, say no to things that will deplete you, and be as kind to yourself as you are to others.*

## Message

Burnout is an epidemic, but you have the power to halt it. Set firm boundaries around the behaviour you'll accept to protect your energy, time and emotional strength. It can be challenging at first—so many lingering feelings of obligation and guilt—but you'll strengthen this skill through practice, and by understanding how precious your time is and how finite your emotional resources. Release the pressure to toughen up or grow a thicker skin to deal with difficult situations or people — it's up to others to respect your parameters.

Reinforce your barriers and focus on what you need, rather than making other things and people the priority. This is *not* encouraging you to say no to everything, cut yourself off from others or be cruel or dismissive — just set sensible limits and express how you'd like to be treated. It's about self-care not selfishness, and is vital for emotional and physical wellbeing. It will also give you more time to do what you're passionate about, be with those you want to be around, and prevent the resentment that can twist into bitterness if you repeatedly do things you don't want to.

Be patient with yourself as you begin setting boundaries. It can take time to unlearn your conditioning and reject the behaviour you've always accepted. You may like to surround yourself with white light or healing energy as a barrier to other people's negativity, or rehearse what you'll say to those you feel pressure to appease. Keep your refusal brief and to the point. You don't need an excuse or explanation, or anyone's permission, to honour your needs.

Most people would prefer you be honest, and horrified to know you're doing something you don't want to just because they asked. And if someone is upset by you setting boundaries, that's on them, and says more about their lack of respect for you than anything else. No one is entitled to your undivided attention or acquiescence. You deserve to have your time and energy honoured, and will be happier and more productive once you insist on it. Make sure you respect other people's boundaries too. Most are quite clear about what they want, so pay attention to what they're saying as well as their physical cues.

# Helpful Deities

Call on the Lady of Avalon, a Celtic goddess of transformation, who represents the ancient feminine energy of the realm of Avalon and of the earth. She is the fierce protector of her own sovereignty—and of yours—and can be worked with to set limits and develop the confidence to ensure your needs are met. You can also work with Artemis, the Greek goddess of protection and the hunt, who will lend you the strength to create firm boundaries, say no to people and things that will drain you, and erect barriers for protection from hurt and trouble.

# Affirmations

No is a complete sentence.

My boundaries are strong and clear.

I am forthright, frank and honest in my speech and intentions.

No is not a bad word.

Saying no to one thing allows me to say yes to something even better.

# 3. The Gift of Yes

*Embrace a new opportunity or challenge yourself to try something you're not sure you can master. Powerful change comes from stepping outside of your comfort zone. Take a chance, summon your strength and say yes to something you've been longing to experience.*

## Message

No can be a powerful word, but so can yes. There are times when setting boundaries and protecting what matters to you by saying no is the perfect response, but at other times, a yes can be just what you need. Be brave and agree to do the thing you fear. Summon your courage and take a risk. Follow your curiosity to see where it leads. Push yourself out of your comfort zone and feel yourself soar. Say yes to the things you love doing and the people you long to be with, rather than allowing the best and most precious things to be what you keep sacrificing.

Pick one thing you want to do that you'd usually say no to, and do it. An invitation, a request for help, a daunting opportunity — if you feel yourself about to refuse, stop, and say yes instead. It might be awkward or annoying, or it could be life-changing. Sometimes forcing yourself to face a fear will be the thing that breaks its hold over you. You might meet a new friend, conquer a fear, find an activity you love, blossom as you work on a passion project, explore a new career path or discover something new about yourself.

Waiting until you feel ready to face a challenge can mean you never do it, leading to deep regret. How many times have you wished you'd said yes when you had the chance? How much longer will you hide your capabilities, and watch as others grab your opportunity and run with it? Changing your automatic no to a yes will shift you to a growth mindset, broadening your mind and increasing your possibilities and potential.

Embracing yes and being open to new experiences can deepen connection with family and friends too, reawakening your sense of adventure and joy. It gives you the space to try, fail, learn and grow. It removes some of the fear and risk, and encourages you to follow your dreams. At first you may be nervous, even scared, but keep going. Leap out of your comfortable existence and let the act of doing push you through fear and out the other side. Rather than overthinking it and psyching yourself out, stand in your power and choose to take action with courage and conviction.

# Helpful Deities

Call on Sekhmet, the lion-headed Egyptian sun goddess who embodies the strength of that regal creature, who can help you develop the confidence to face new challenges, and the courage to leap out of your comfort zone. Sekhmet's name means 'the powerful one' or 'the mighty one', and she can be worked with as you start to be honest about what you want in life, open up to trying new things, and for protection and healing. You can also invoke the Sumero-Babylonian goddess Ishtar, for strength, bravery, the power to face your fears and cut through obstacles to your goals, and the self-assurance to try new things and embrace saying yes.

# Affirmations

Yes!

I can do this.

I'm ready to make the most of this opportunity.

I can do hard things.

I flourish and blossom by opening up to new opportunities.

# 4. Grow Your Gratitude

*It can be easy to feel overwhelmed by challenges and world events. But don't let despair crush you or stop you from taking action. Focus on the good things in your life and give thanks for each one, so you can nurture and grow the sparks of hope.*

## Message

A simple way to bring light and hope to your life is to practise gratitude, focusing on the things that are going well for you. This doesn't discount the darkness or any challenges you're facing, but if you place all your attention only on those, your mood will lower, your light will dim and your negativity will grow. Shift your attention to the good in your life instead, and that's what will increase, as joy can be contagious, and kindness begets kindness.

It doesn't take much effort to start seeing the world in a new way. Keeping a gratitude journal or simply making a note of your blessings in a work diary or calendar can help you see the magic in each day. Appreciate every experience you have—even the tough ones, which often provide wisdom, strength or insight—as well as every chance you're offered, every gift you're given, every person you know. Gifts aren't just things either — there's the gift of time, the acquisition of new skills, the offers of assistance and the things within you that you can offer to others. Performing an act of kindness for someone else also improves your mood and brings pleasure.

If you despair that nothing good ever happens to you, consciously create moments of joy and prove yourself wrong. Call a friend or arrange a catch-up. Do something pleasurable, be it a beach or forest visit, pottery class or concert. Re-read or re-watch a favourite book or film, make some comfort food, volunteer for a cause close to your heart or submerge yourself in nature.

Noticing each precious glimmer of happiness and writing it down will ensure you remember it, add weight and significance to each joy you experience, and encourage more magic and goodness to flow into your life. It doesn't have to be a massive triumph to feel like recording it —

the little things are just as worthy of gratitude. And once you've acknowledged what you're grateful for, create a ritual of appreciation that is meaningful for you, then pay it forward in some way. Appreciating what you have, and giving thanks for it in a way that makes sense to you, is a beautiful way to live.

# Helpful Deities

Call on Hestia, the Greek goddess of kindness and compassion, home and hearth, who represents contentment and joy. Work with her in crafting a ritual of gratitude to help you focus on the good in your life and see the silver linings even on cloudy days, and find ways to pay forward your good fortune. You can also give thanks to any god or goddess you work with, expressing your appreciation for their blessings and your hope that they will continue.

# Affirmations

I am grateful for the good in my life.

I celebrate my blessings.

I embrace an attitude of gratitude.

I give thanks and radiate my blessings outwards.

I appreciate the lesson in this experience.

# 5. Live Your Magic

*Everything you need is already within you. Recognise your wise inner self, nurture your powerful connection with source, and accept all of who you are. Create the life you dream of by kindling your spark of enchantment into a roaring flame.*

## Message

There is magic within you, waiting for you to connect with it and start weaving together the life you want. Waiting for you to take a step forward, to stand in your power and declare to yourself, and the world, who you are and who you want to be. Waiting for you to realise that the power to create and change your life and your self is your birthright. Waiting for you to claim your magic, expand your truth, and see the beauty and wisdom within you.

There is magic in everything. In nature, science, learning and people. In stories, travels, animals and the earth. Real magic is the magic of the everyday. The magic of family and friends, of the strength found in community, and of the bonds you weave with the people who have your heart. There's no need for smoke and mirrors, magic tricks or illusions. You can weave your own spells with your intent and your passion. Craft your own life with the depths of your heart and soul.

You have as much magic within you as anyone else. Your visualisation of the outcome and your choice of words, your charging of the ingredients or tools with your own energy, your intent in casting — all of this is what makes the magic happen, is what gives a spell or ritual its power. *You*. Don't give away your power and agency to anyone, no matter what promises they offer or sweet words they speak. Instead, recognise these qualities within yourself, and acknowledge and embrace them. As above, so below. As within, so without.

Open your eyes as well as your heart to see the divine in the world around you, then notice it reflected within yourself, and embody it in your daily work. If you're not happy with some aspect of your life, change it. Make it different. Make a difference. Speak the truths within your heart.

Embody the power and strength within you, as well as the vulnerability. Be all of who you are, and all you want to be. Don't just see the magic in every day, *be* the magic. Step into your power and your passion. Find the warrior within you, the sorcerer, the seer, and connect with your inner enchanter so you can radiate your light ever outward.

# Helpful Deities

Call on Hekate, the Greek goddess of witches and spellcraft, night and the moon, to help you understand your own innate magic and connect with its power. A light-bringing torchbearer, she illuminates the darkness so people can find their own wisdom. As a crone goddess, figure of fate and an aspect of the triple goddess, Hekate is associated with the waning moon; she's a deity of initiation, prophecy, magic and mystery, who sends visions and dreams to those who seek them, and seek her. You can also work with the triple god and triple goddess to introduce yourself to the breadth of perspective and enchantment at your fingertips and coursing through your veins. Or choose a pantheon and take time to connect with each deity to explore how meaningful they can be in your life.

# Affirmations

I connect with my inner magic.

I stand in my truth.

I am powerful and strong and capable of creating the existence I desire.

I channel the magic of nature and the energy of the earth.

The most powerful spell is my life.

With my intent, I create miracles.

# 6. Focus On the Also

*Each of us has a galaxy of moods, emotions and abilities within, and a balance of light and dark. Even in the depths of despair, know you are never just that. There are always glimmers of hope to be found if you remember how many positive traits you have, and all the wonder you hold within you.*

## Message

You're a different person to everyone you know, showing different parts of yourself depending on how you perceive them, while those around you will see different things in you according to your interactions with them and as reflections of themselves. This means you can be different people and live different lives, trying out hopes, dreams, goals, values and personalities by spending time with a variety of people, so you can discover which *you* that you like best, who you want to be and who you truly are.

You are a unique galaxy made up of bits of lots of other people — the love of reading your grandma instilled in you, the cheeky spirit born from a sibling relationship, the dedication your favourite teacher inspired, the politics of a parent, the career path inspired by your greatest rival at school, the love of nature gained from a friend, regardless of whether you're still in touch. Consider the people in your life, those who have influenced you in some way, and be sure they are positive traits you have taken on, ones you still want in the star-strewn sky of your heart.

You are so many things all at once, and are capable of being even more, and it's important to remember this, especially in dark times, when you're struggling to see any light. An emotion or situation can sometimes be so overwhelming and all-consuming that, for a while, it's all you feel and express — if you're sad, angry or filled with shame, it can seem as though that's all you are. That every bit of your light and joy is drowned in the sea of shame or pain. But it's not true. You can be consumed by sadness, *and also* still be kind and funny and clever and sweet, even if you don't feel it in that moment. You can be burning with anger or jealousy, *and also* still be a good friend, a good parent, a good person. Whole universes dwell within you, and you can embody them all. You are *always* all of you, even when you don't feel like it at the time, and this is true for everyone else as well.

## Helpful Deities

Call on Rhiannon, the Celtic goddess of love, the new moon, rebirth and transformation, to help you work on issues of self-trust, self-knowledge and inner strength. Let Rhiannon remind you that you are stronger than you think, inspire you to discover your own way to survive—and to survive with joy—and eventually thrive, after a situation that seems terribly bleak. Also known as the night queen, Rhiannon was falsely accused of a terrible crime by her people and unjustly treated by her husband, but she endured her punishment with patience and love, grace and dignity, confident that truth and balance would eventually prevail — and she forgave all those who'd wronged her once it did.

## Affirmations

I am enough, always.

I shine my light outwards even while sad.

I can conquer darkness, hurt and loss.

I am many things all at once, and feeling sad or angry does not diminish any of them.

I am a universe of possibilities.

7. Stop the Spiral

# 7. Stop the Spiral

*Make an effort to broaden your outlook. You have the power to flip this situation on its head and see it in a new, truer way. Rather than zeroing in on the negative, soar above to widen your perspective, and consciously remind yourself of all the positives.*

## Message

When something unfortunate happens, it's easy to slip into a spiral of negativity and believe bad things always happen to you and nothing ever goes your way. But focusing only on the things that back up this belief turns your false belief into a self-fulfilling prophecy. The brain relies on you to determine what is true or false. It can't process everything, so it searches for patterns and what it thinks you want to focus on. When you're happy with a friend, partner or situation there's no drama, but if they hurt you or let you down, your brain starts recalling similar instances, or looking for new ones, and will overlook all the good things as they don't fit the new narrative. The more you spiral into doubt and suspicion, the more your brain will amplify every tiny negative incident.

If a friend lets you down, you can focus on other times you've felt this way and doubt your entire relationship, or smile as you remember all the good times and brush this incident off as an exception. If you make a mistake at work, you can dredge up other times you erred and panic you'll be fired—or even leave as a pre-emptive move—or take a deep breath, make amends, then continue confidently on. There are even times when a misunderstanding or outright lie underpins your new negative belief, so be sure of the truth before you react and punish the other person or yourself.

If you find yourself stewing in worst-case scenario thinking, force yourself to stop, remind yourself that your brain is fixated on the worst interpretation, and consciously flip the script to focus on positive moments or memories. By all means, allow yourself to feel sad or disappointed by what happened, but don't blow it out of proportion, allow it to define your entire relationship or make you give up a person, situation or dream you love, especially if it's based on an untruth. If every interaction with them is awful, of course you should leave or challenge the status quo, but don't sacrifice something wonderful because one minor glitch has affected your perception and painted everything black when it should be rosy.

## Helpful Deities

Call on Athena, the Greek goddess of wisdom, intelligence and clear thinking—or her Roman counterpart Minerva—for assistance and discernment with the situation at hand, and for encouragement with strategic planning and careful thought. She can help you understand other perspectives, temper irrational emotions and avoid catastrophising one small worry into a misperception that leads to a deluge of unwarranted negativity. Athena, who was the patron of Athens, emerged fully grown from her father Zeus's head, linking her to wisdom and the love and pursuit of knowledge.

## Affirmations

I see this situation clearly.

I will focus on the whole, and keep things in perspective.

I weigh things up fairly and dismiss minor annoyances.

I'll be calm and choose how to react.

I embrace the power of perspective.

# 8. Change Can Be Good

*When you have an opportunity to walk a new path, embrace it wholeheartedly. There can be incredible gifts in learning new things, great joy in transformation, and whole new worlds to inhabit when you challenge yourself to stretch and grow.*

## Message

It's time to get out of your comfort zone and embrace change. It can feel difficult, even threatening, to transform an aspect of your life, find a new dream or adopt a different viewpoint, and some people may belittle you for doing so. But "you've changed!" is not an insult; it's the highest form of compliment. Don't let anyone place limits on what you can do, believe or be, and don't do it to yourself either. Loving your life and where you are is wonderful, but if you're feeling stuck, miserable or discontented with any part of it, open yourself up to the possibility of something new and allow yourself to transform.

You may be essentially the same person you were as a teenager, might care about the same issues and have broadly the same morals, but every year, every *day*, you discover so much more. Sticking doggedly to your adolescent worldview and holding to beliefs that no longer represent you can be harmful — there are some things you *should* change your mind about. You learn about yourself, and are influenced and opened up to the world, from the people you meet, by reading and studying, by your everyday lived experiences and by being open to the possibility that other ideas, opinions and viewpoints are just as valid as yours.

You may even realise you've been wrong about some things, and that's good. That is growth and insight and courage. It's drinking from the cauldron of wisdom and integrating all that you learn therein. It's discarding the layers you've been protected by and stepping out of the shelter of your cocoon, so you can blossom into all the beauty and light you can be.

Embracing change is a powerful way to honour yourself and your progress. To emerge from the expectations of others and find a unique path, hard-won and all your own. And as you unfurl your butterfly wings and celebrate this, gift others the space to change their minds and their beliefs as well — to work through issues and experiences so they can learn, grow and develop into the person they are meant to be, discovering what is true for them too.

## Helpful Deities

Call on Ceridwen, the shapeshifting Celtic goddess of rebirth, transformation and inspiration, for support in making a change and rewilding, renewing and reinvigorating your life. Associated with the waning moon, you can invoke her in her aspect of crone and elder, to uncover your inner wisdom, develop prophetic foresight and help you release what is holding you back from learning and growing. This wise crone goddess can guide you as well as challenge you — it can be hard, deep work, but it is always worth it. Like other dark moon deities—including Kali, the Cailleach, Hekate, Baba Yaga and Nephthys—Ceridwen can help you descend to your metaphorical underworld to examine your shadow, heal and integrate all your parts, and emerge stronger, lighter and renewed.

## Affirmations

I value new wisdom and seek new knowledge.

There is power and joy in transformation.

I enthusiastically embrace change.

Changing my mind is a strength, not a weakness.

I see this ending as a new beginning.

# 9. The Power of Silence

*Speak your truth and have honest discussions. But listen to others too. Take time to shut out the noise of the everyday world so you can start to hear your inner voice and understand the longings of your own heart and soul.*

## Message

Silence can be restorative and empowering, or isolating, condescending and passive-aggressive. Sometimes it speaks more powerfully than any words, and you'll connect to your inner wisdom if you learn to embrace its gift. If you're not used to silence—if you always need music on, or a TV or radio playing in the background—it can be confronting to sit with the discomfort of no sound. Long-ignored thoughts, fears and questions may surface, the ones usually covered up by noise and chaos. Discovering your deepest feelings rather than burying them unheeded can be challenging, but it's worth it to deal with them and begin to heal.

You will benefit from time alone to connect with the guidance of your heart, and the inner voice and intuitive wisdom that is part of you. So switch off the sounds of modern life and reflect. Slow down. Meditate. Breathe. Walk in nature as a sacred pilgrimage. Surrender your need for action and achievement. Feel your way into the silence. Ponder. Become comfortable with periods of quiet and inaction, with blocking off time to process what you're experiencing, make sense of your current situation, and discover how you really feel.

Can you be quiet yourself, and hold your tongue, or are you uneasy with pauses in conversation, blurting out the first thing you think just to fill them? There's wisdom in waiting until you're sure you want to voice your thoughts, admit your fears or spill your secrets. You can always share something later, but once spoken, words can't be withdrawn or unsaid. When you practise sitting with silence, you will learn to not automatically fill any gaps in a conversation, and discover the power of your voice when used at the right time, in the right way.

Be conscious about your silence though. Don't refuse to speak as a form of punishment or part of a game.

Giving someone the silent treatment in retaliation for a perceived hurt or as a way to 'win' is cruel. There are times when misunderstandings can only be unwoven through the vulnerability of speaking your feelings and discussing the issue. And don't allow anyone to silence you or make you feel you can't express yourself, or do it to anyone else either. Listening is an underrated skill, and everyone's voice is important.

## Helpful Deities

Call on Sige, the Gnostic goddess of silence, to gift you the blessings of quiet and deep thought, of connection to your inner wisdom, and of understanding the power that not speaking can have. Considered to represent the void from which all emerges, she is thoughtful, primordial and deep, asking you to retreat, rest and restore your energy, recharging from the intensity of modern life with time in silence and contemplation — even if it's just 10 minutes alone under a tree or hiding in bed with the covers pulled up over you.

## Affirmations

I embrace the silence, and welcome the insights it provides.

I relish quiet time to just be.

I value the inner voice I hear when the surrounding sound is muted.

I love the clarity of my thoughts when I can hear them.

My feelings turn up when the volume is turned down.

I will talk less and listen more.

# 10. Impress Future You

*Instead of feeling overwhelmed and giving up on your dream, drill down on exactly how to make it happen, then do something towards it every day. Even small daily achievements soon add up, creating momentum to keep you inspired, and showing your progress — progress that your future self will thank you for.*

## Message

Time has become a little strange of late — days blending into each other, a year passing in the blink of an eye yet also feeling like a lifetime. This time distortion makes it difficult to look ahead and picture where you want to be a year from now, two years — or even just next week. As past, present and future blur, goal setting can be challenging. But creating a routine and focusing on a positive future has been shown to improve wellbeing and provide light and hope when darker memories swirl. Meditation, mindfulness practices and structure can help settle time misperception and ease anxiety, and taking action provides a sense of control.

If you're putting things off until you have more time, or more will and intention, think about what you want to achieve, and how good it will feel once you hit your goal. Visualise the result very clearly, then envision the future you who has achieved it. What did you do to get there? Break it down into small, actionable steps, and write them down in the order required. Instead of waiting until you have lots of spare time (a myth!), do one small thing every day. It may not seem like much at the time, but each action will add up. Learning five words of a new language each day might sound pointless, but do it every day for a year and you'll be able to get around in a foreign country. Writing a hundred words a day doesn't feel like much, but it's achievable, and within 12 months, you'll have a novella. Most things worth having take time and perseverance, and daily habits that will push you towards your goal.

Don't shame yourself if you haven't begun yet; just make a plan and dive in. Set some deadlines, or make yourself accountable to someone. And don't be discouraged.

No one naturally has discipline; it's a skill you have to learn and turn into a habit. Just take consistent daily action, acknowledge each step you've taken, and allow your progress to spur you on. A year from now, you will wish you'd started today, so make your list and do one thing right now. Future you will thank you for it.

## Helpful Deities

Call on Minerva, the Roman goddess of wisdom, clear thinking and intelligence, to help you make a plan and stick to it, and guide you into becoming consistent in your efforts. She is associated with strategic planning, dedication, philosophy and victory, and is the counterpart of the Greek goddess Athena, another deity of determination. Minerva was said to have emerged from her father Jupiter's forehead—the seat of thought—fully grown and ready to fight for what she wanted.

## Affirmations

I am committed to my goals.

I will make future me proud.

Small steps are important.

Every day, I am becoming the person I want to be.

My future light begins from today's tiny spark.

# 11. Out of the Darkness

*Reconsider what you gain by hiding your light, denying your joy and keeping your expectations low to avoid disappointment. Know that it is safe to express your shadow side and release your pain. It's time to kindle the spark of light within you into a beautiful flame.*

## Message

Sometimes it can be tempting to stay in the darkness, to only focus on the hopelessness and helplessness you're drowning in, because it feels comfortable there. Familiar. When you remain closed down and wallowing in sadness, despair and pessimism, there's no risk of failing, no pressure to shine and sparkle, or give of yourself, because you don't even try. You fool yourself into thinking you're content, and safe, but checking out of your life is *not* about safety or protection. It just means you'll stay home, stay small and stay as you are. That you'll hurt yourself so no one else can hurt you first — even though no one was going to.

Perhaps you're gaining something from letting bleakness and negativity define you. The attention you receive because people are concerned about you might be sustaining you — and making you scared they'll no longer care if you're happy. So you reject companionship and happiness before anyone has a chance to reject you, pretending you're content with things as they are. But remaining in darkness is not improving your life, keeping you safe or protecting you from pain. It's not saving you from potential rejection or heartache; it's simply preventing you from finding love and joy and reaching your goals. And the longer you shun the light, the harder it will become to emerge from the shadows.

Stop using this place of misery and stasis as an excuse to not pursue your dreams. Throw off the limits you've imposed on yourself, emerge from the darkness and look for the light. Sometimes it just takes a slight shift of perspective to see it. To realise that the only true failure you'll suffer is when you don't even try, the only real regret you'll feel is for all the things you *don't* do, and that your friends won't like you any less when you are your shining self again, but will love you even more. So step out of the darkness you're stuck in and start to nurture the tiny spark within until it's a sustaining flame. It's time for you to grow and learn and shine your light, throwing off the shackles of the expectations weighing you down.

## Helpful Deities

Call on Theia, the Greek goddess of light and vision, who helped humans see the radiance of the world, and can assist you in seeing your own light and beauty. As the deity who endowed gold, silver and gemstones with their brilliance and lustre, she's associated with all that shines, as well as being linked to the stars and the night sky. She is mother to Selene, the moon goddess, Helios, the sun god, and Eos, the dawn goddess, so you can work with her at any time of the day or night to bring divine light and clear seeing into your life. Daughter of Gaia, the earth mother, she's also connected with clairvoyance, able to help people see ghosts and spirits, and was known by some as Euryphaessa, which means 'wide-shining'.

## Affirmations

It is safe to move forward.

I will shine in the light.

I am worthy of love, whether I'm happy or sad.

People care about me because they like me, not out of obligation.

There is value in darkness, and integrating it within me.

# 12. Find Your Familiar

*Animals hold much wisdom and strength, and can be a source of great love and comfort. Whether it be your own animal companion or a more spiritual form you connect with through meditation or metaphor, allow them to provide guidance, consolation and healing.*

## Message

The soothing purr of a cat, the comforting companionship of a dog, the peaceful sight of fish swimming in a pond or birds dipping through the air — animals can be a great source of stress relief. Guide dogs have long helped the vision-impaired, and more recently, therapy animals—from dogs and cats to horses, guinea pigs, birds and snakes—have played vital roles as companions to people with autism, anxiety, depression, PTSD and addiction, amongst other conditions. Some dogs are so connected to their human they can warn a person with diabetes when their blood sugar has dropped too low, and many animals provide incredible emotional support to those in need, as well as love and devotion.

Just being around animals can be deeply healing, whether it's with your own beloved companion, the wildlife in your local park, working at an animal rescue centre or visiting a cat cafe. Spend time with a furry, feathered or scaled friend, allowing them to uplift your mood, soothe your soul and share a lesson of love, comfort and simplicity. Learn about the native animals in your area, taking note of their life cycles and migration patterns and finding wisdom within these, and check whether any need to be protected.

Many magical practitioners have a close spiritual bond with an animal—their familiar—working with them in rituals and communicating with them psychically and emotionally. Some energy healers have even found their animal friends wanting to help them, placing a paw on the patient's shoulder to add their healing to the treatment.

You can also build a relationship with an animal spirit guide for support, divination and healing. You may have a primary guide, as well as communing with different ones at different times and for different purposes. Connect through meditation or shamanic journeying, by drawing them, writing to them or crafting a ritual, visiting them at a zoo, wildlife park or in the wild, reading about them, keeping pictures or photos of them around you, singing or chanting to them, studying their characteristics and habitat, sitting outside and calling to them, or campaigning on their behalf through wildlife organisations or a specific group that works with that animal in the physical world.

# *Bonus: Some Friendly Familiars*

An animal may come to you through signs, symbols, dreams or ritual work, or you can establish a connection by approaching the animal you feel most drawn to.

- **Bee:** A reminder of life's sweetness, and the importance of loyalty and teamwork, and sharing your burdens.

- **Butterfly:** A symbol of joy and transformation, to lift the spirits and reassure you that change is a wondrous thing.

- **Cat:** To summon courage and independence, balance the light and dark within you and without, and relax and connect with yourself.

**Deer:** For gentleness and kindness, especially to yourself, and the grace to endure difficult circumstances with sensitivity.

**Dove:** A divine messenger who will bring you peace, love and hope.

**Firefly:** For inspiration and hope, as it brings light and life to the darkness.

**Fox:** For flexibility, creativity in finding solutions, and the confidence to change and grow.

**Hummingbird:** To bring a higher vibration, and for love, joy and lightness of being.

**Kangaroo:** For strength, leadership and decisiveness, and a reminder to keep moving forward in the direction of your dreams.

**Otter:** For joy, laughter and lightness, to connect with your subconscious and your inner child so you can play, and to foster optimism in hard times.

**Owl:** To connect with your inner wisdom and explore the mysteries, seeing beyond the surface and into the darkness to learn the truth.

**Raven:** For journeys of self-discovery and transformation, and to uplift your mood and inspire you to new heights.

**Snake:** To connect with your intuition and follow your instincts, and prepare to let go of—or shed— something that no longer serves you.

# Helpful Deities

Call on Freya, the Norse goddess of love and war and mistress of cats, who sometimes rode a boar and other times a chariot pulled by cats; Bastet, the Egyptian goddess of love and fertility and mother of cats; or Lady of the Beasts, the cross-cultural goddess of animals and wild places who protects all living beings, including you. Work with them to connect more deeply with your own animal companion or to find a familiar to do magical work with. You can also help rescue or heal an animal you feel a connection with, which might involve financial support for endangered animals you can't visit, or adopting a rescue pet and lavishing as much love on them as you will receive in return.

# Affirmations

I open my eyes to the animals around me and welcome the messages they have for me.

I will protect and care for the animals of the world.

I honour the wisdom of animals and pay attention to their lessons.

I appreciate the simplicity and joy of creatures, and will bring these qualities into my life.

# 13. Listen to Your Heart

*You deserve to be happy, and to pursue the things that bring you delight. You don't have to wait until you've achieved or earned anything to justify it. Honour the things that are meaningful to you, that lift your heart and spirits, and make time to do them more often.*

## Message

What is in your heart? What are you longing to do? What do you *not* want to do? In the busyness of life, it's common to sweep your dreams and desires under the rug and out of sight, vowing to pick them up again "one day". But too often, this mythical "one day" never comes, and the call of the things you yearn for slowly softens then fades away, until you no longer hear it at all.

Yet, burning within you is the light that makes life meaningful, that can show you the way through the darkness when doubt and sorrow encompass you, keep your spirits up when things feel too hard, and give you purpose amongst the humdrum of the day-to-day. If you've lost track of what brings you joy, or forgotten how to nourish your soul, it's time to find it again and reconnect with this vital part of your self. It might be something simple, or huge and elaborate. It could be a single idea, or many. Don't overthink it; just recall a time you felt genuine pleasure, and commit to revisiting it this week.

If there's something you'd like to try—a new hobby, class or place to explore—do it. Having a fulfilling career you love is wonderful, but if not, use your downtime to pursue what nourishes you. Is there something you're jealous of or about in others? Envy isn't a negative emotion *if* you use it as a tool to discover what to add to your own life. Coveting what someone else has or does provides important information, revealing what you long for. Be brave enough to acknowledge what's missing, what you've lost or let go of, and make the effort to regain it.

There's no time to squander, no justification to wait — instead, make the most of every precious moment you have, while you have it. Turn your dreams into reality, and make sure you schedule breaks so you can relax and re-energise too. You deserve to be happy and fulfilled. To work hard, then enjoy your downtime. To prioritise friendship and love, and time with people you care about. To listen to the deep yearnings of your heart, and honour them.

# Helpful Deities

Call on the Three Charites, or Graces, of the Greek pantheon—Aglaea (Shining), Euphrosyne (Joy) and Thalia (Blooming)—who represent happiness, love and the coming of good times, and who lift the hearts of those who connect with them. They are associated with light, charm and goodwill, and are connected with Aphrodite, the Greek goddess of love. The meaning and symbolism of the *Three of Cups* tarot card has been linked to the Three Graces, symbolising the ability to embrace authenticity and your true self, and radiate joy and positivity outwards as well as within.

# Affirmations

I deserve happiness, and to pursue it for its own sake.

My joy benefits myself as well as everyone I come in contact with.

I listen to my heart's yearning, and act on it.

Being happy is worthwhile for its own sake.

I know what lights me up, and I do it often.

14. What Are You Waiting For?

# 14. What Are You Waiting For?

*Don't wait for others' permission or a lack of obstacles
before making a start on what you really want to achieve.
You get what you work for, not what you wish or wait
around for, so begin taking action towards your goal today.*

## Message

What's your dream worth to you, and how badly do you
want it? Blaming other people, circumstances, events or
lack of time for not achieving the results you crave is giving
your power away. It's up to you to reject excuses and make
it happen. No one is coming to do the work for you. No one

else will get out of bed early, write out your business plan, create that product, learn the skill, forge that path or take a risk for you. It's entirely in your hands, which is scary but also empowering.

Some days will feel easy — ideas will flow, inspiration will swirl around you, and you'll make great progress. Other days will be harder, tempting you to give up, but those are the times that define you. Sticking with it when you're tired, when progress seems non-existent, can be the thing that leads to your big break, or the difference between passing or failing. Many people abandon their quest when it gets tough, right before they would have succeeded. But not you. Honour your dreams, as well as the journey you're on to reach them, and celebrate the downs as well as the ups, knowing you'll learn even more from the challenges than the triumphs.

It's never too late to change an aspect of your life. You decide where the line is between what you want and what you're willing to do to get it, and how far out of your comfort zone you'll venture. When things become difficult, remember your why, focusing on the goal and how amazing it will feel to reach it. Whatever it is that you hope for, don't wait around for things to happen to you, or for decisions to be made by others. *You* get to choose what to make of your life. To decide how to spend your time, who you want to be, and who you want to be with. Don't give your power to others to define you. Don't be invisible. Show up in your own life, and show up for yourself. Fight for what you want, put in the work, the energy and the effort, then celebrate when you achieve it.

## Helpful Deities

Call on Artemis, the Greek goddess of the moon and the hunt, for help with focus, clarity and determination. Known as a protector of women, girls and animals, she's the wild woman of nature and the woods, who shoots the arrows of truth and can thus guide you to uncover your own inner truths, then pursue them with unerring aim until you hit your goal. She can assist you in deciding what you want and encouraging you to go after it, increasing your confidence, starting to appreciate your independence and nurturing your needs and interests.

## Affirmations

I am worthy.

Now is the time.

I'll keep working until I reach my goal.

I honour my dreams.

I am in control of my life.

I make things happen.

# 15. Let Down Your Guard

*Building walls around your true self can make you feel safe, but it can also keep you locked away and disconnected, living a smaller life than you have the potential for. Be courageous; lower your defences, embrace vulnerability and show your true heart to those who matter to you, and see your whole world open up.*

## Message

While it's tempting to always put forward your best self, and hide your supposed flaws and fears, true intimacy requires vulnerability, sharing and deep feeling, and a willingness to be emotionally and metaphorically naked. It's time to let your armour drop and allow your vulnerability to be seen. You've spent so long with your heart protected by swords, hidden behind impenetrable walls, but it's safe to let them fall and let someone in. You don't have to reveal your inner self to everyone, or share every thought or secret. Just disclose to those you trust deeply, and take it as slowly as you need.

Being vulnerable is not a weakness; it's a strength, allowing you to examine your life in a new way. Sadly, many people were raised to believe vulnerability is a fault, yet it's an incredible gift, both to yourself and any person you offer it to, because it takes courage to risk breaking through barriers and revealing your true self. And it can be incredibly rewarding, transforming relationships and bringing you closer to people. It can also empower others to share their own inner selves, sparking healing and growth in them, and increasing your connection. So don't let a harsh world shut you down and stop you letting people in, and helping them lower their armour too.

The first step in embracing vulnerability is to become aware of the things you've worked so hard to keep hidden, possibly for years. The secret fears and worries you've buried beneath layers of shame and denial, the behaviours you regret and despair over, the beliefs you've taken on — that you're too difficult, too much, not enough, never good enough, a fraud, a fake, an imposter. Acknowledging these shadowy parts of yourself will help you understand your fears and insecurities, and in doing so, hold them up to the light for healing. In recognising, labelling and integrating your vulnerabilities and anxieties, you'll realise they were never as bad as you thought. Everyone has areas they feel vulnerable in, and being able to accept yours, work on them and share them will inspire others to shine a light on their own and start doing the shadow work you've been brave enough to begin.

## Helpful Deities

Call on Diana, the Roman goddess of light and the moon, and protector of the vulnerable, to help you reveal the hidden parts of yourself, and release any shame you're holding on to, knowing she will hold you safe and protect you emotionally as you dare to bare your heart. An embodiment of the full moon, motherhood, the earth and creation, you can invoke warrior goddess Diana, and her Greek counterpart Artemis, for support as you open up, inspiration to guide you on how to best express your vulnerability, and for courage, confidence, and physical and emotional strength.

## Affirmations

I am enough just the way I am.

Sharing my heart with others is empowering for both of us.

I embrace the gift of vulnerability with strength and courage.

I will speak my truths in gentle ways.

Those who hear me will appreciate me sharing, and baring, my soul.

I embrace all who reveal their own vulnerabilities, and honour their bravery.

I offer the gift of my vulnerability to those who deserve it.

# 16. Laugh in the Face of Adversity

*Laughing prompts your body to produce feel-good endorphins. Cultivate some humour and happiness—even if it feels less than genuine at first—to make yourself laugh and lighten your heart and your life. Bonus: it will cheer up those around you too.*

## Message

It's said laughter is the best medicine, and while not technically the *best*, there is some truth to the sentiment.

Not only does laughing stimulate your heart, lungs and muscles, it also boosts the feel-good neurochemical dopamine, lights up the reward centre of your brain, improves immunity, increases resilience, and relieves physical and emotional stress by lowering cortisol and upping serotonin. It stabilises blood pressure, releases endorphins, lessens chronic pain, and induces the brain waves experienced by regular meditators. Laughter forces you to remain present too, and is highly contagious.

And you don't have to actually *be* happy to laugh. Your body can't distinguish between real and fake laughter, so whether genuine or not, the act of laughing will make you feel happier. So laugh in the face of adversity, knowing even forced laughter will lift your mood. Laugh when you're stressed, and feel the tension leaving your body, since its effects are the polar opposite to the body's stress response.

Of course, happiness doesn't mean the absence of problems, sadness or responsibility, and there will always be challenges in life, painful moments and obligations to fulfil. Laughter won't fix them, but it will help you cope better, and change the way you react. Laughing about a stressful situation can make it easier to deal with, and can help reframe a sad or negative story as a funny anecdote you'll laugh about later with your friends, such as the terrible travelling experience that becomes the highlight of your trip when you recount it, and the thing most fondly remembered.

The pursuit of happiness is not about chasing it, but practising it and experiencing it, and fortunately, it's an emotion you can cultivate. Studies show that people who have close relationships, volunteer, stay healthy and active, have a sense of spirituality (be that from religion or a connection to nature), practise gratitude and make time for hobbies are happier than those who don't. It's also been found that children laugh about 400 times a day, yet sadly, adults only manage 15. So dive into your child-like wonder and curiosity, reach out to your friends, form a community, do something you love, no matter how silly, and recapture the joy that is your birthright.

## Bonus: Love to Laugh

Laughter therapy, also known as laughter yoga, uses humour as a nonpharmacologic way to improve wellbeing. There are classes both online and in person, with many different instructors so you can find someone you resonate with. You may feel a bit silly at first, but practising with others will forge a wonderful connection, and the endorphins will soon kick in and drown out any self-consciousness.

You can also do it alone, right here, right now. Try a small, shy giggle to start with. Then a short, slightly bashful chuckle. A longer, louder chortle or a gleeful cackle. And a deep, increasingly genuine belly laugh. (I tried it, and while I did feel a little silly at first, it works!)

If you need something more tangible to get started, watch a funny movie or a favourite sitcom, go to a comedy show, read a light-hearted book, stick comic strips to your fridge, start a jokes notebook and record any that amuse you, bookmark silly videos, recall an embarrassing situation, pull faces at yourself in the mirror or call your funniest friend.

## Helpful Deities

Call on the Greek god Gelos, the divine personification of laughter and companion of the revelry-loving Dionysus, to lift your mood and fill you with the capacity for joy. Or, invoke his fellow deity Baubo, the goddess of mirth who is renowned for her bawdiness, jesting and refusal to take herself seriously, and was the only one who could make Demeter laugh amidst her grief at losing her daughter to the underworld. You can also work with Euphrosyne, the goddess of joy and mirth, whose name comes from the Greek word for merriment, and who is one of the Three Charites or Graces.

## Affirmations

I radiate joy.

I deserve to be happy.

I embody laughter and spread it around.

I cultivate humour as a light in the darkness.

I laugh at adversity and choose to focus on delight.

# 17. Turn the Page

*It's okay to move forward and chart a new, more fulfilling course. Honour the things you've achieved, the efforts you've made and the chapter that's ending, then leap into the next one with joy and excitement.*

## Message

Someone or something is holding you fast, stuck in a situation or headspace you want to move on from, and it's tearing you apart. Whether you got talked into it, chose it yourself, ended up here by accident or were deceived in some way, you need a solution, because life is too short to be doing things that stress you out, make you miserable or pull you away from your true joy and purpose. You don't have to stay in a bad situation, fulfil an obligation you regret agreeing to or remain in an antagonistic relationship, and nor should you — it will drag you down, blotting out the light and hope you should be surrounded by with the heavy weight of duty and resentment. But you have the freedom to choose to move forward, change or remove yourself from a situation you've outgrown or is causing you harm, and seek joy and fulfilment.

First, make the decision that you want to break the chains and turn the page, because your intent is powerful, and will fuel the changes required. Then brainstorm the best way forward. You may be able to remove yourself from the situation, rewrite the deal or change an aspect of it so it works better for you. If you must fulfil it this time, either legally or because you're getting something out of it, promise yourself you won't accept anything similar again.

Don't despair about the situation or curse your weakness for agreeing to it. You can learn a great deal from a less-than-ideal experience, so try to see all the good you can take from it, and be grateful for this new knowledge. Integrate the lessons and growth, appreciating all you've gained, then reflect on the chapter you're bringing to an end, celebrate what you achieved, and be excited about the chapter to come. Vow that you will pursue what you want, and say no to the things you don't. You have control over your own life, and the power to be your most effective advocate and make the best decisions for you — decisions that will lead to happiness, growth and purpose. So release your fears, resentment and sense of obligation, and turn the page so you can step into this bright, light-filled new future.

## Helpful Deities

Call on Isis, the Egyptian goddess of alchemy, transformation, and initiation into the Mysteries, for strength to make the changes you long for, and the courage to contemplate and pursue something you never imagined for yourself. Considered the divine mother and giver of life by those who worship her, Isis is a nature deity, the patron of magic, healing and spiritual science, and is even credited with inventing marriage, through her union with Osiris, the god of death and the underworld. Isis remains a symbol of enduring, eternal love because of her devotion to her husband even after death. Fellow deity Set, the god of storms, war and chaos, murdered Osiris out of jealousy at the power he wielded and the love their people felt for him, after which Isis resurrected her husband — just as you can resurrect a new life, and a new chapter, from the place where you are currently stuck.

## Affirmations

I have the power to change this situation.

I am in control of my life and my actions.

I will turn the page and start a brilliant new chapter.

I embrace joy and pursue happiness.

I move forward confidently into the life I long for.

# 18. Fail Forward

*Don't allow your fear of failure to hold you back. Failure can be one of the most important steps towards success. Even if you doubt you'll be able to hit your mark, be brave enough to try. Value any so-called failures as wonderful lessons and the impetus for another attempt.*

## Message

Despite the natural tendency to want to hide mistakes, it can be empowering to accept and celebrate them instead. Embracing failure is now recognised as a key to hitting your goals, because rather than being the opposite of success, failure can actually be its foundation, fuelling you to continue, pushing you to try harder, and providing vital insights, lessons and experience. Those who've been wildly successful, from inventors to pop stars to business people, know failing is part of the journey, and they often learn more from it than from success.

Without taking a chance and risking failure, you'll never know what you're truly capable of. Instead of pre-empting the outcome and not even trying, commit to the effort, and be proud of your courage and hard work, no matter the result. Fortune favours the brave. You can decide not to apply for your dream job because you're convinced you won't get it, or put in your application and see what happens. End a relationship at the first sign of disagreement, or be vulnerable and work through the problem. Throw in your fitness goals after falling off the wagon, or give yourself grace and restart the next morning. You have nothing to lose by trying, or by failing, and everything to gain.

If it doesn't work out this time, don't be discouraged. So-called failures are just a small part of the total journey, and can inspire new methods, new ideas and new paths. Failure is only regrettable if you refuse to learn from it and try again. Don't let your fear hold you back from pursuing the things you want, be put off by the criticism of people who don't even have the courage to try, or rob yourself of the opportunity to take a chance and experience new things. People won't laugh at you for trying something; they'll applaud you for having a go. They might even be inspired to get past their own fears and try something too. Let go of self-criticism, embarrassment and worries over being judged, and get excited by failure. It gives you somewhere to go, a goal to fight for or task to complete, and it builds your character, resilience and tenacity — the bedrocks of lasting success.

# Helpful Deities

Call on Ceres, the Roman goddess of determination and the earth, to help you pick yourself up and move forward after a setback, and start to see failure as an offering of precious new knowledge that will increase your resilience and capability. Like her Greek counterpart Demeter, Ceres didn't stop looking for her daughter Proserpine until she found her, continuing relentlessly in the face of repeated failure and setbacks, until she was finally able to rescue her from the underworld, albeit for only six months of each year.

# Affirmations

I am brave and will keep trying until I succeed.

I embrace so-called failure for the lessons and experiences it gifts me.

I am eager to take a risk.

I will succeed eventually, and enjoy the journey along the way.

Failing forward is still a step towards my goal.

19. Give Yourself Grace

# 19. Give Yourself Grace

*Start treating yourself with the respect and kindness you grant everyone else, and forgiving yourself for the small things you tolerate without question in others. Be proactive in moving through the stress and overwhelm that darkness can bring, and cut yourself some slack, refusing to sweat the small stuff any longer.*

## Message

Being let down by someone you trust or having to turn the other cheek at work can be hard to deal with, but unless it's a regular occurrence, most people forgive mistakes and move on. But do you find it impossible to forgive *yourself* for the same 'crimes'? If you're berating yourself for doing—or not doing—something, consider how you'd react if a friend or loved one had done the same. Would you be angry and vengeful, or forgive them without question? It's time to be as kind and forgiving to yourself as you are to others.

Stop punishing yourself and being your harshest critic. It's not fair, and it's also not helpful. Berating yourself for procrastinating won't inspire you to work harder; it'll just send you into a spiral of frustration, depression and more procrastination. Instead of pouring on the self-loathing, lighten up on yourself. You don't have to be productive every day. If you're feeling stuck or uninspired, take a break. Replenish your well. Do something that nourishes your soul and fills your heart with joy. Your passion and desire will return, but in the meantime, give yourself the grace you offer everyone else.

This isn't an excuse to continue slacking off or behaving badly, or free rein to forgive yourself for something but not make amends to the person you upset. You still need to take responsibility for your actions and examine the situation objectively, working out if there's a way you could improve things—and doing it, if so—or whether it's your attitude to yourself you need to adjust. If you're stuck in overwhelm and burning out, pause, take a deep breath, and change the situation. Accept your limitations with patience and understanding. You don't have to do everything for everyone, so decide what's most important, then let go of the things that don't matter so you can take care of the things that do. Accept when you need to say no to things, and learn how to do it. Renegotiate and change your circumstances when you must. Success is not about getting everything on your to-do list done, but having the discernment to work out what is necessary versus what you can cross off and leave undone.

# Helpful Deities

Call on Hathor, the Egyptian goddess of protection and healing, who was also celebrant and mistress of the cycles of time, and linked with fate and forgiveness. Revered as the mother of the pharaohs and a mother goddess, she ruled love, joy and music, and was kind, protective, nurturing and devoted. The Greeks associated her with their own Aphrodite, and you can work with both of these goddesses for help developing self-love and compassion, encouraging self-care practices and increasing your spirit of generosity to encompass yourself as well as others.

# Affirmations

I forgive myself as I forgive others.

I release self-judgement and self-criticism.

I embrace acceptance and self-compassion.

I aim for progress, not perfection.

I am enough.

# 20. Stand Your Ground

*Examine your beliefs and the values and ethics you hold dear. Ensure that you're not compromising who you want to be in order to impress someone or avoid conflict. It can be uncomfortable, but you need to back yourself and fight for your convictions when they are important to you.*

## Message

It's okay to go along with the desires of your family, partner or friends occasionally, when you don't mind the outcome or are happy either way. But when it comes to the important things in life, don't allow yourself to be swayed. Stick with your principles. Refuse to give in on the fundamental issues and beliefs you hold dear in order to impress someone, gain their approval, or receive applause or a promotion. Don't condone something that doesn't sit well with you—or even just watch it happen silently, without protest—be pressured into doing something you know is wrong or violates your principles, and don't let anyone silence you.

This is not the same as arguing just for the fun of it, being arrogant and stubborn, or remaining so wedded to your opinion that you refuse to acknowledge that someone else's view might be equally valid. But when you face a tough choice and have to decide between what is right and what is easy, do what you know in your heart you should, rather than compromising to avoid conflict or benefit in some superficial way. Back yourself, and others, when you know it's the right thing to do, speak up for those who are vulnerable—including yourself—and don't be swayed by peer pressure or family influence.

It's not always simple — core values are different for everyone, depending on upbringing, experience and education, and there's no one you'll agree with on absolutely everything, even your best friend or partner. Sometimes disagreement is healthy, and you'll both learn and grow from discussions. But if it's something fundamental to your very being, you'll need strategies to cope. Research the issue so you can speak confidently when making your point. Practise what to say so you don't get tongue-tied. And, depending on how important the issue is to you, be okay with limiting your interaction with the person or even letting them go.

Who you are is forged in the tiny actions you take and decisions you make every day, and acting contrary to your values can damage your self-esteem and your relationship with yourself. Discover what's non-negotiable to you and honour your true self, connecting with your inner strength and power, and asserting your worth.

# Helpful Deities

Call on the spirit of Blenda, the Swedish battle queen, or Boudicca, the British warrior queen, for strength and courage in asserting yourself, speaking your truth and standing up for what you believe in. They protected their people, spirituality and way of life with conviction, and you can channel their confidence and gentle yet fiery strength to do the same for yourself.

# Affirmations

I am stronger than I think.

My principles are important and worth speaking out about.

I am a priority.

I don't need anyone's approval.

My boundaries will be respected.

# 21. Ask What Is Meant

*When you're unsure about something, avoid assumptions and request clarity around meaning and motives. Determine whether someone is acting in response to you, or as a result of their own issues. Not everything is about you, and not all burdens are yours to carry.*

## Message

Would you rather believe a lie because it makes you feel better, or discover the truth, even if it hurts? Do you find yourself assuming the worst about someone's actions, taking them as a personal slight, when they may have nothing to do with you? People aren't mind readers. You need to tell them how you're feeling, and what you want and expect from them. Equally, you must ask for clarity when you don't understand what someone is saying or you're confused about their actions and the meaning behind them. Most things people do are not related to anyone else, so don't automatically take it personally or invent motives that don't exist.

If someone says something upsetting, don't immediately jump to conclusions. Instead, hit pause on your hurt and ask them exactly what they mean. They may be mortified that you interpreted their words the way you did, and be at pains to reassure you of what they intended. Or they may have meant exactly what you thought, but at least you'll react from a place of knowledge. Don't take someone's silence as an answer or sign either — they may have no idea you're waiting for a response. If you want to know what someone's feeling, be brave enough to ask. It's all too easy to be misunderstood, and if you assume the wrong thing and respond angrily, frostily or with silence, they may get the wrong idea too, with things quickly spiralling out of control.

Be patient. Not everything is about you. Don't assume someone is acting in response to you or your actions. They may be completely oblivious to you, wrapped up in their own concerns — perhaps even something you could help them with, if you take the time to ask rather than imagining it's your fault they're upset and spinning off to a catastrophising conclusion. Don't guess how people will react either, or assume that what you find unacceptable will be a deal breaker for others. Gently let people know the behaviours and actions that are non-negotiable for you so they understand what you expect, and ask for theirs. Your lists will rarely match, and it can be illuminating to realise just how differently you see the world. It will also save a lot of heartache to be upfront.

## Helpful Deities

Call on Calliope, foremost of the Greek Muses and known as the goddess of clear communication, for help in getting what you mean across, expressing yourself well and avoiding confusion and miscommunication. Calliope, whose name means 'beautiful-voiced', is in charge of writing, music, song and dance, is the patron of epic poetry, the source of inspiration to writers and poets, and the deity who assisted humans to express what is in their heart with truth and eloquence — a quality you can channel today.

## Affirmations

I will ask for clarity instead of assuming.

I express my own needs clearly, and explain my actions and motives.

I acknowledge that not everything is about me.

I value clear communication in others as well as myself.

I release the burdens that are not mine to carry.

# 22. On the Threshold

*A wonderful opportunity has just opened up, and the possibilities are endless if you can be brave enough to move forward and grasp them. There's no need to be afraid — it's just a doorway, so step through with confidence and embrace this chance.*

## Message

You're standing on the edge of a great opportunity, and have the ability to make the most of it, if only you can find the courage to leave what is comfortable and safe, and step forward to embrace it. Let go of your fears and anxieties, square your shoulders and summon your strength. It's just a door, after all — turn the key and walk on through. One step after another until you find yourself on the other side, and forget what you were ever worried about.

There is power in thresholds, magic in liminal spaces, and in the prospects and potential they represent. In this moment you are one person, but you are on the precipice of becoming another. In a single moment, you can dream of something else, and *be* someone else. The world is alive and shimmering with possibility, and it's up to you to take advantage of it and not let it pass by. It doesn't have to be a huge life change you're stepping towards — there are small doors to move through too, and myriad chances to step up, to meet someone new, to learn a skill and to challenge yourself to grow.

You don't need to have all the answers or know every step of the journey towards your goal before you commit to crossing the threshold to pursue it. Just dare to take one small step, and then another. Open the door. Peer through it. Adjust to the light and the temperature and the idea of you being there. Thriving there. Have faith that you are capable of handling this new challenge, choice or situation. Learn as you go, figuring out what's needed when you get to each new circumstance, and facing everything with confidence and the wisdom already within you. It's okay to be nervous and unsure, even scared, of what it will mean to grasp this opportunity, but don't let that stop you. You are strong and brave, and you deserve this. Tell your fear, doubt or hesitation that you don't care for its opinion, and ignore any excuses it throws up. Disregard any negative comments from people around you too — you're capable of achieving your dream and deserving of success, so step through this doorway into the light of this new day and allow yourself to shine.

## Helpful Deities

Call on Janus, the Roman god of doorways and gates, duality, choices, beginnings and transitions, to allay any fears you have of what it will involve and what you're up against when you challenge yourself to graduate to the next level. Depicted as having two faces, Janus can see into the past and the future at once, as well as seeing different sides and being able to weigh up options before making a decision. So he can help you see further ahead, through the doorway and into the wonderful opportunities you're being offered. You can invoke the Greek crone goddess Hekate too, who also rules doorways and crossroads, as well as the liminal space between where you are now and where you are capable of going. Gather your strength while you pause there, then ask for their wisdom and guidance as you embark on this new journey and embrace the chance being offered to you.

# Affirmations

I am ready to take this step.

I am grateful for the opportunity to move forward.

I'm excited to see what is on the other side of this door.

I embrace this threshold and am excited to cross it.

I welcome change and can't wait to turn the key.

# 23. Nurture Mind, Body & Spirit

*Nourish and care for your physical self as well as your mind and soul. To thrive instead of just surviving, tune in to your emotional, mental and physical health, and nurture yourself before you feel depleted.*

## Message

It's time to check in and ensure you have a healthy balance in mind, body and spirit. Consider how you feel physically, how well you're doing emotionally, and whether your spiritual side is being nurtured. All three are necessary for wellbeing, for each impacts the other. You can't be as emotionally strong as you'd like if you don't have good physical health—and vice versa—and feeling at peace spiritually is vital to overall health too. Don't beat yourself up if an area is currently lacking; just commit to improving it.

Are you getting enough sleep, eating well most of the time, drinking water and incorporating daily movement? You don't need to train for a marathon, mountain climb or bodybuilding contest (although you can!). Just add some activity each day — a nature walk, dancing, yoga, ocean swim, fitness class, team sport, anything that makes you feel happy and alive. Exercise isn't about punishing your body or yourself, but making it stronger and more capable of housing your spirit, so you can do the things you want to do. Everyone has their own physical issues, challenges and limitations, so work with what you have and do what you can, knowing the stronger you feel physically, the stronger you'll feel emotionally, and the more energy you'll have to pursue your goals and follow your dreams.

Are you paying enough attention to your emotional, mental and spiritual health? If you have unresolved anger at a person or situation, make the effort to heal it. If depression, anxiety or trauma are impacting you, be brave enough to seek help, because you deserve to be cared for and feel nourished, whole and happy. If you lack purpose, get to the heart of what you want to achieve, then take steps in that direction. Perhaps meditation or energy healing will boost your mood and focus. If you're religious, leaning into that can provide comfort and spiritual sustenance, or it may be in helping others or spending time in nature that you're fulfilled. Just know how important you are, how vital all aspects of your health are to your experience on this planet and your ability to embrace life and love, and how deeply you deserve to feel joy and wholehearted wellness.

## Helpful Deities

There are many deities who focus on healing, it being such a crucial area of life. You can call on Asclepius, the Greek god of healing and medicine. His daughters Hygieia, a goddess of physical and mental health, and Panacea, a goddess of healing, can also be called on for strength, willpower and wisdom on your healing journey. Additionally you can work with Airmid, the Irish goddess of herbs and healing, Brigid or Bridie, the Celtic goddess of healing, fertility and motherhood, and the Greek and Roman god Apollo, who ruled over good health and healing along with many other aspects.

## Affirmations

I honour my mind, body and spirit.

I strive for full health.

I look after all parts of my being.

I deserve vibrant health.

I am healthy and strong, and my mind is clear and focused.

# 24. Magic of Stories

*Share your story, and allow others to share theirs with you.
We understand ourselves and the world through personal
and archetypal stories, so express the words written on your
heart in order to share who you are, make connections and
see your whole self.*

## Message

There is magic in words on paper, and voices in ears.
Enchantment in the sharing of experiences that make
sense of a situation. Stories have the power to change
you, challenge your views, remind you of your better self,

encourage empathy, inspire deeper understanding, spark curiosity and wonder, help you understand the world around you, and offer hope when all feels lost. Poets can stir an army to fight and provide solace after a difficult battle. Musicians lift the spirits of those celebrating and help the grieving to process their loss. Non-fiction writers help people feel heard, seen and understood. Novelists sweep readers away into worlds that offer possibilities undreamed, bringing joy to the sad, filling the void for the lonely, and empowering people to escape their own reality for a while.

It's time to express the stories swirling in your heart, share the experiences that hurt or heal you, tell the tales that fire you up, or read what brings you comfort. In dark times, curling up with a favourite book can soothe your soul. When your spirit is low, writing can help ease the pain, whether it's a private journal entry, a public blog, a song or a novel. And sharing your experience by telling someone your story, and hearing theirs in turn, raises awareness, provides a different perspective, and can be transformative for you both.

Whether writing them, speaking them or listening to them, sharing stories can be a revolutionary act, a communication and connection between writer and reader, artist and viewer, singer or teller and listener. Books offer inclusion, characters to love and hate, dilemmas to face and new perspectives to live from. Readers have been shown to have more empathy, be more likely to help someone or support a cause, and be more accepting of difference. Stories, poems, plays, movies and songs encourage creativity, and are a way to understand things more deeply and connect with the world, with friends and with your own inner self. The story of you is a wonderful gift to offer someone, whether it's your childhood hurts, your happiest moments or your deepest wishes. Weaving words, speaking truths and discovering the plot points of your own life will transform you, and allowing your imagination to spark will strengthen your spirit when hope is fading.

# Helpful Deities

Call on Thoth, the Egyptian god of wisdom and truth, for clarity in word and deed. Associated with writing, translating and advising, Thoth was credited with the invention of language, writing, magic and religion. He spoke the words of the sun god Re, who created life, and was a moon deity and the masculine counterpart of Ma'at, the goddess of law, justice, wisdom and truth. You can also work with Seshat, the Egyptian goddess of reading, writing and wisdom, and the deity associated with libraries. She's the sacred scribe who encourages you to learn from the stories of your past in order to improve your future.

# Affirmations

My words have power.

My story is valuable.

I am worthy.

Vulnerability is a beautiful, generous gift.

I embrace the shadow and the light in my story.

Sharing what is in my heart will help others as well as myself.

25. This Storm Will Pass

# 25. This Storm Will Pass

*Life ebbs and flows like the ocean, and change is a vital part of the universe. No matter how tough it feels right now, the dark clouds will eventually blow over, the sea will settle, the sun will come out and the light will return. Focus on what you need to stay calm and the strength and learning that will result.*

## Message

Storms are inevitable, in nature and in life. When faced with the stress of an emotional storm, it can be traumatic, and difficult to imagine your way beyond. But the only constant is change, and no matter how hard it feels right now, even the darkest of storms *will* pass. Try to bend like the willow while the storm rages, biding your time, conserving your energy, and allowing the wild winds not to break you but to strengthen you. Let things wash over you rather than reacting immediately, and practise patience as you wait for it to pass.

Instead of trying to calm the storm, calm yourself. Sometimes all you can control is your own reaction. Remove yourself from the situation, change tack, counter-offer, seek outside advice or determine not to let it get to you. Every storm eventually dissipates, and often waiting it out can be a good way to deal with it, rather than adding fuel to a lightning-fuelled fire. Nurture yourself while the storm rages, and in its aftermath. Do things that bring you joy. Rest, soak in a bath, meditate. Regulate your fear response, inhaling then exhaling slowly and intentionally. When the storm dies and peace returns, look at the world washed clean and discover the strengths and insights you gained. Many who've weathered their own tempest choose to be kinder and more compassionate, and you may emerge with new wisdom and resilience, an understanding of your limits and strengths, and better prepared for the next storm — or able to sense it coming so you can reach shelter in time.

Another option is to become one with it. Channel its energy, and ability to impact each thing it touches. Let it crash over you and revel in its strength, absorbing it and bracing yourself to better cope with future upsets. Embrace its wild power. Sometimes, when your life is spinning out of control, it's a message you've chosen the wrong path, and an encouragement to seek new purpose and meaning. This storm could be moving you in a different direction, pushing you to purge your life of people or situations that are no good for you, or get rid of excess baggage and emotions that no longer serve. So metaphorically toss them overboard, and revel in the freedom, calm and lightness of being.

## Helpful Deities

Call on Yemaya, the West African and diasporic water goddess who rules love and healing as well as oceans, rivers and lakes. She is a mother goddess, the giver of life and love, a fierce protector of the oceans and other water bodies of the planet, and is sometimes depicted as a mermaid. Also associated with the moon and thus emotions, Yemaya is nurturing, nourishing and protective, offering abundance, comfort in trying times and peace in the storms of life.

## Affirmations

This storm will pass.

I am capable of surviving this temporary challenge.

I see the silver lining in these thunderclouds.

I embrace the chaos and allow it to push me forward.

I can weather any storm.

I *am* the storm.

# 26. A Poisoned Arrow

*Holding on to a grudge is more damaging for you than the person it's aimed at. For your own sake, it's time to release your bitterness over the past or present so you can start to heal, and move forward with lightness and joy.*

## Message

Bitterness is a toxin that snakes through your body, slowly destroying you from the inside — and the worst part is that it's *you* who loosed the arrow that's piercing your heart and infecting your soul. The person responsible probably doesn't even know how you're feeling, and isn't impacted.

Instead you're the one left seething with resentment, unable to escape the sting and move forward, and unwilling to deal with or heal the self-inflicted fury.

You're allowed to feel angry with a person or situation, or yourself. But either use it to fuel action that will bring about a resolution, or find a way to release it. If you stubbornly hold on to your rage, repressing your emotions and stewing in silent resentment, it will fester, poison your heart, and affect your physical and mental health. This doesn't mean your feelings aren't justified. Bitterness grows out of hurt and betrayal, from an injustice, real or perceived, and it's not unnatural to want the culprit to hurt as much as you're hurting. But this bitterness only affects you. The person who caused it continues on, oblivious to your pain, while you suffer the toxic impact emotionally, physically and spiritually.

Acknowledge your feelings so healing can begin. Signs of bitterness include replaying a situation over and over, fixating on something someone did long ago, keeping score of every offence—real or imagined—and finding yourself annoyed by everything someone does because your perception of them is so twisted. Investigate the cause of your bitterness. It could stem from a misunderstanding, a false assumption or something beyond anyone's control, in which case you can let it go. If it *is* justified, try to resolve it. This could involve communication—does the person even know they're upsetting you with their actions?—counselling, setting boundaries around what you'll accept, or removing yourself from a situation or relationship for your own peace.

Step out of the pool of bitterness before you drown. Holding a grudge requires an incredible amount of energy to sustain and casts a deep shadow on the grudge-holder, and clinging to something you can't change just gives the person who hurt you space in your head. Make the effort to let your resentment go and forgive — for your sake, not theirs.

# Helpful Deities

Call on Tara, the Hindu and Buddhist goddess of forgiveness, compassion and wisdom, to help ease your bitterness and show you how to gently release it so you no longer suffer from its toxic pain. Recognised in some regions as a bodhisattva and in others as a female buddha, Tara's name is Sanskrit for 'star', reflecting her purpose of shining her light to guide people along their spiritual path and towards enlightenment. She encourages the letting go of human suffering, is a protector and mother figure, and works selflessly to bring peace and contentment to all. She appears in many forms, including Green Tara, who is associated with the moon, enlightenment and active compassion, and White Tara, who is concerned with peace and long life. You can also work with Clementia, the Roman goddess of forgiveness, mercy and clemency for yourself and others.

# Affirmations

I release this bitterness.

Other people's actions wash over me without impact.

I am free of resentment and perfectly calm.

I let go of pain and suffering, and breathe in peace.

I forgive this person for my own sake.

These actions no longer affect me, and only reflect on the person doing them.

# 27. Progress Not Perfection

*Don't get derailed from what you dream of doing by too-high standards and fear disguised as procrastination. Make an effort to take the pressure off and enjoy the process, knowing that done is better than perfect, because perfect never gets done.*

## Message

How many amazing projects have you started, but given up on because you're convinced they're not good enough? How many opportunities have you turned down through insecurity and fear? The idea of perfection can be the enemy of progress, so put aside your hesitation and get something finished and out there. Too many people refuse to show anyone their art, story, music or dreams; they baulk at trying for a promotion, taking a risk at work or entering a competition, worried they're not good enough, not perfect. But *nothing* is perfect. You could spend your whole life revising and reworking something, with no guarantee you'll like it better even if you do one day finish it, and risk that you'll edit out the spark that makes it unique. Or you can put it out into the world and start working on something new.

Perfectionism is part of an all-or-nothing mentality that inhibits your progress and prevents you from even beginning. It can make you miserable, stressed and frustrated, lead to burnout, anxiety and depression, missed opportunities and envy towards those who get things done. It will rob you of joy and satisfaction with what you do achieve, hinder creativity and imagination, and show up as procrastination, where you're so scared you won't do a brilliant job that you don't even start. Instead, focus on progress, not perfection. Rather than allowing your high standards to paralyse you, give yourself grace and just do your best. You are enough. Accept yourself and your capabilities. This isn't to say you should hand in unfinished work or not make any effort, but a well-done project completed on time is worth far more than a so-called perfect one not submitted at all.

Enjoy your life, enjoy your journey, and celebrate your progress and effort. Say yes to the things you really want to do, joyfully create what's in your heart, and know participation can be more valuable than mastery. Challenge yourself to be happy with good enough, happy with done, and show your art, submit your project and say yes to that opportunity you longed to take up but didn't. Embrace any mistakes or seeming failures, enjoy the process of learning and growing, and let that spur you on to make your dreams come true, one perfectly imperfect moment after another.

# *Bonus: Action Tips*

- Terrified of speaking in public? Do it anyway. A waver in your voice or a stumble over your words will endear you to most listeners, not make them critical.
- Not putting your hand up for a promotion because you don't think you're ready? Apply regardless. Many people less qualified than you will, and one of them will get the job because they put themselves forward and you didn't.
- Obsessing over an assignment or project so much that you don't even submit it? Get it in. Even a lower grade than hoped for is better than a fail because you didn't hand it in.
- Too insecure to sign up for a yoga class or go to the gym because it looks too hard? There's no shame in modifying an exercise so it works for you, or staying in the beginner class forever. The only way to get better is to *do*.

# Helpful Deities

Call on Airmid, the Irish goddess of healing, herbs and hidden wisdom, to help you surrender your perfectionism and embody grace and patience. A member of the magical Tuatha De Danann, she was generous with her healing skills and sought peace amongst her family and her people. You can also work with Guanyin, the Buddhist goddess of compassion, kindness, mercy and love, for the strength to step out of your comfort zone and pursue what brings you joy, regardless of your current skills.

# Affirmations

My best effort is valuable.

I am enough.

I release the beliefs that are limiting me and the pressure I'm putting on myself.

Progress is more important than perfection.

Getting it done is better than getting it perfect.

28. The Hurt You Hide

# 28. The Hurt You Hide

*Never be scared to reveal your hurt and pain. Honour it all, and work through it in your own time, being honest about the ups and downs. Sharing your pain will let the light in and help to heal your heart.*

## Message

Whatever is hurting you right now—the loss of a loved one, a relationship, a period of life now over, a career you loved, an idea that didn't pan out—be patient with yourself. You don't have to open up to a new life, new love or new dream on anyone else's schedule. Allow yourself to ache and burn, to be breathless with the pain. There's no shame in showing your grief — don't lock it away so other people feel comfortable. Honour your needs. Whether you'd rather be alone or you crave companionship, no choice is wrong. And don't buy into anyone else's idea of what your behaviour should be. Perhaps a temporary withdrawal from life, work or love is what's necessary, or maybe getting right back out there again will help you most. It's up to you.

There's no right or wrong way to express pain or grief. Resist those who pressure you to move on according to their timetable, or push you to do anything you feel uncomfortable about. You don't have to return to your usual life yet — or you may be ready before others deem it appropriate. Listen to your own heart. Healing isn't linear, so allow the bad days, and bad moments, to be expressed, while holding tight to the good ones. Don't feel guilty for finding happiness in the small joys of life amidst your heartbreak, for they can co-exist. In faery tales, tears have power and magic to heal illness and create transformation. They are therapeutic in the real world too, so allow yourself to cry if you need to, and feel yourself being cleansed physically and emotionally. Movement can also help move stuck energy through your body, so walk or dance or run or swim or do some boxing to rebalance and reconnect with your own body and self.

It's no consolation, but it's a blessing to have a love, life, job or dream that's mourned when it ends. The person, situation or experience has changed you, and will be part of you forever. Take comfort in remembering what you had, what you built, and what lives on in you, even after your loss. Treasure what it gave you and who it made you. And know there is help and support if you need it.

# Helpful Deities

Call on Morrigan, the Irish and Celtic goddess of death, sovereignty and guardianship, to help you come to terms with your pain and loss, and eventually, when you are ready, to start to feel the warmth of the sun, the comfort of supportive loved ones and the possibility of a new future as she gifts you hard-won strength. You can also invoke Kali, the Hindu goddess of life, death and destruction, who is known as the mother of all and the giver—and the taker—of life; Greek deities Thanatos, the god of death, and Hekate, the goddess of cronehood, death and the underworld; and Hel, the Norse goddess of the underworld and leader of armies.

# Affirmations

I acknowledge my pain and allow myself to feel it.

I am grateful for the love I was honoured to give and receive.

I choose my own timetable and begrudge no one their own.

I honour my grief, and hold on to the beauty of my memories.

I appreciate the lessons hurting has taught me.

# 29. Threads of Fate

*Take control of your own destiny and become an active participant in your life. Claim your agency by making the big decisions based on what you want, not what others expect of you. The power to choose is yours. Stand strong and weave each strand of your story, making sure it's the one you want to live.*

## Message

Some people believe fate is preordained, and there's no point fighting it. That some other force spins the thread of your life, creates the tapestry of your existence, then snips it off at the end. You can use this as an excuse to stay stuck in a bad situation and allow life to simply happen to you, or recognise that you *do* have control. You have the ability to make decisions, take action and change your trajectory if you're not happy. Some things, like family, are fixed, but you can still adjust your dynamic with them if necessary. You can't alter the education you already have, but you *can* learn whatever you want now, be it from life experience, books, courses or returning to study, and you can choose a new career if you're called to. You can set boundaries for the behaviour you'll accept, improve your health and fitness and thus your quality of life, transform your outlook and become the person you want to be.

Empowering yourself by taking responsibility for your actions means you choose your fate. You decide your purpose, your work, your relationships and your lessons. Refute expectations about what you're capable of, don't rely on other people's views to define you, and ignore their opinions on what you should do or be or want. Knowing each day and each choice is up to you avoids self-fulfilling prophecies too, because if you don't like a prediction, an expectation or a family trait, you can ensure it doesn't come to pass. You're in control, accountable to yourself for your happiness and satisfaction, and can launch a new future at any moment.

With this power comes responsibility, so consider how closely your actions reflect your words. It's easy to say you care about an issue, just make sure you're backing that up, because it's not your words that define you, it's your actions. Just like love being a verb not a noun, an action rather than a proclamation, live what you say. Claiming to care about an issue while doing nothing to improve the situation makes the prettiest of words a lie. Be the person you want to be, that you say you are. Weave your own fate, craft your own tapestry, and create a life of magic, joy and intention.

## *Helpful Deities*

Call on the Moirai, the three Greek goddess sisters who control the threads of life, and ask for their wisdom and encouragement as you weave the strands of your own life to create the tapestry you dream of. Also known as the Fates, they are the personifications of destiny — Clotho spins the thread of life onto her spindle, Lachesis measures the length of each thread, and Atropos decides the manner of each person's death and cuts their thread and thus their life (a heavy responsibility!). To the Romans, they are the Parcae, and to the Norse, they are the Norns, believed to represent the past, present and future.

You can also call on Arianrhod, the Welsh mother goddess of the full moon and motherhood, who is associated with the silver wheel, the stars and the sky. Patron of fertility, childbirth and maternal nurturing, she weaves the webs of fate and destiny, and can be invoked for wisdom, inspiration and deep inner knowing. Her Greek counterpart Ariadne, goddess of the shining moon and stars as well as the dark underworld, is also associated with destiny and fate, as well as mazes and labyrinths, healing and emotional development.

# Affirmations

I am creating my own life.

I have control over my choices.

I'm responsible for weaving my own fate.

I choose how I react to what happens to me.

I have the courage to take charge and make things happen.

30. Allow Yourself Rest

# 30. Allow Yourself Rest

*Carve out some time today to relax and recharge. You deserve it, and you also need it, physically, emotionally and mentally. You can only perform well, live well and be well if you are in good health.*

## Message

Productivity at all costs has become a modern-day mantra, with bosses expecting 24/7 availability and more output with less staff. As a result, many treat it as a badge of honour if they're first into the office and last to leave, or the one offering to work weekends. Being a workaholic has been so glorified that it's now considered normal. But it's not. Being dedicated and working hard is great, but it can turn toxic if taken to extremes. Don't let your self-worth be so bound up in doing and pleasing that you sacrifice everything for a job or person.

If you're constantly overwhelmed, exhausted and under pressure, make time to rest. Schedule it if you have to. Small amounts of stress can focus your mind and help you power through a task, but only in short bursts, and only if it's followed by adequate restoration. Being constantly and chronically stressed is dangerous, raising cortisol levels, increasing blood pressure, impacting immune and adrenal systems and causing digestive issues, muscle tension, migraines, insomnia, chest pain and even heart attacks. It affects you emotionally too — you may suffer from depression, brain fog, memory issues, inability to concentrate, cope or function, lack of motivation, and a constant sense of dread, overwhelm and burnout that stifles your ability to hear the cues your mind, body and spirit send.

You don't have to be doing things all the time to have worth. Your value is not defined by overtime, overwork or overproduction. You don't have to hit a target or prove anything to anyone to be deserving of love, respect or time out. Challenge the narrative that your worth is linked to your output. In the short term, naps, breathing exercises, meditation, mindfulness, physical activity and removing yourself from stressful situations will help. You'll also need to set boundaries and safeguard your time and energy.

Don't work yourself into a health crisis because you believe that's the only way to be seen as valuable. Nothing is worth your health or wellbeing, so embrace the concept of radical rest, make time to sleep, and give yourself permission to relax. Change your life and your habits now, rather than waiting for a health scare or a terrible loss to force you to realise your priorities.

# *Helpful Deities*

Call on the gentle Hypnos, the Greek god of sleep—whose name was used to describe hypnosis and hypnotherapy—so he can ease you into a restful, dream-like state that is restorative and deeply healing. He utilised his melodious voice to induce gods and mortals into a trance state, possibly the first recorded use of hypnosis, the psychological practice of guiding someone into a deeper state of consciousness to relax completely, recover memories and improve focus and concentration. Once Hypnos or his Roman counterpart Somnus have given their assistance, you can work with one of the warrior goddesses such as Andraste, Bastet or Freya to help you create boundaries around your time and say no to the things that are draining you physically and emotionally.

# Affirmations

I am worthy, no matter what I do or don't do.

Taking time to rest and restore is sacred.

I seek balance and an even keel.

My boundaries are healthy and strong.

I deserve to relax and recharge.

31. What Drags You Down

# 31. What Drags You Down

*It's time to release what no longer brings you joy, and embrace who you are in this moment. Growth and change are normal and positive, but can be challenging. Letting go of something heavy will be a blessing.*

## Message

Something's holding you back and dragging you down, so release it and move forward with lightness, confidence and joy. It might be a situation you have to leave, a decision you've been avoiding, or a relationship you need to reassess. It can start with the merest hint of dissatisfaction,

a slight unease when you're with someone, or a vague
suspicion that there's more to life — but if you don't address
it, it could snowball until you're so miserable it feels like you
have to upend everything and escape your entire life just to
feel well again. Often, you already know what must change
and just have to take action, but if you're not sure, spend
some time in quiet reflection, journalling to make sense
of things, walking in nature to spark epiphanies, going
through old photo albums to trigger a breakthrough, or
using a divination tool to find clarity.

If it relates to your sense of purpose, taking up a hobby to
channel your passion into may be enough, or you might
prefer to explore a new career path. If it's possessions
or financial commitments dragging you down, refining
or tidying might boost your mood, or it could require a
complete overhaul of what you do or how you live. If it's a
relationship of any kind, try spending less time with them
and adjusting expectations when you meet — unless being
with them is so detrimental to your wellbeing that you
must end your connection and move forward separately for
your own mental health.

None of this means a relationship, job or situation was
always terrible. Once it may have brought you joy and
comfort, addressed your needs and been enough for you.
But habits, hobbies and interests you previously loved
may no longer fulfil you, so stop doing them and use the
extra time to discover what will make you happy now.
Relationships don't have to last forever to be important —
people change and grow, and sometimes grow apart, and

that's okay. Breaking up with a friend or partner doesn't negate the wonderful times you had or the gratitude you still feel for all they brought you. But if something is dragging you down and preventing you from living the life you dream of, let it go and revel in the calmness, joy and peace of honouring who you are in this moment.

# Helpful Deities

Call on the Mayan moon goddess Ixchel (also known as Lady Rainbow), who is often depicted as the triple goddess in her aspects of maiden, mother and crone. She's the mother of the earth and its people, of the moon and the waters, and patron of healing, weaving, childbirth and destiny. Ixchel will help you release what no longer serves you, what is dragging you down and keeping you stuck, and prepare you so you can invoke Aine, the Celtic goddess of summer, sovereignty and the moon, who lights the way forward for those who seek a new path, and will lift you above the things holding you stuck.

# Affirmations

I release what no longer serves me.

I step forward into freedom.

I embrace what brings me joy in this season of my life.

I honour the changes within me, and honour them within other people too.

I cast off the pettiness around me, and seek the higher good.

# 32. Embrace Uncertainty

*In divisive times, it's easy to fall into an echo chamber of people with similar views and simply reinforce each other's positions, never challenging or being challenged. Listen to different viewpoints and encourage debate, question what is true, and change your mind when you learn new things.*

## Message

People are becoming increasingly polarised and divided. More certain of the righteousness of their position, and less willing to listen to any other view. Ready to go to war, figuratively speaking, on the flimsiest pretext, and prepared to pass judgement on someone else's say so, without checking the facts. It's a dangerous way to live, causing suspicion, hurt and exclusion. It also prevents progress and the ability to move forward meaningfully, and backs people into a corner where they're fighting so hard to defend their position that they refuse to concede there's an opposite view, let alone that it could have merit.

It's okay to admit you don't know everything. There's so much information—and disinformation—and not enough time to examine every issue in depth. It's perfectly reasonable to concede that you were naïve in the past, unaware of the full story, or swayed by someone you admire. It's a good, brave thing to change your mind when you realise someone was misrepresented. To reverse your position on an issue you passionately believed in when new facts come to light. Give up on a dream if a new one becomes more important. Refuse to take a position on something if you don't feel qualified to comment.

Be curious when people disagree with you. Try to see their side, even if just as an intellectual exercise. Two seemingly contradictory things can both be true at once, so ask questions and test other perspectives. There's much to lose in not considering another view, and so much to gain by opening your mind, exploring possibilities, and being kinder in your dealings with those you disagree with. Don't compromise your principles, but learn from people who draw different conclusions to you.

Finding a way forward that incorporates everyone's concerns and is the least harmful option has been lost. When talking with someone who holds an opposing view, pause your defensiveness and listen to them. Consider that they might have a valid reason for their opinion. Everyone gains if judgement is withheld until all have been heard. Be courageous enough to have uncomfortable conversations and question your own motives, as well as those of others. If nothing else, it will mean you can calmly and clearly articulate your own position.

## *Helpful Deities*

You can work with Ma'at, the Egyptian goddess of law, justice, wisdom and truth, or her masculine counterpart, Thoth. Both will help you weigh up issues, balance understanding and examine truth. Ma'at, the personification of law and morality, keeps chaos at bay, regulates the cycles of time, and is the feather that balances the scales of the dead. The principle of justice, as well as a goddess, she is shown as a woman with an ostrich feather for her head. Thoth is the god of the moon, sciences, sacred texts and magic, and is believed to control space and time.

# Affirmations

I am open-minded and open-hearted.

I seek new information and other views.

I am eager to learn more.

I acknowledge that I don't always have the right answer.

I am committed to ongoing conversations and explorations.

# 33. Slay Self-Doubt

*You are your own toughest critic, but with a shift of perspective, you can become your biggest cheerleader. Instead of focusing on your flaws and allowing doubt and fear to dictate what you do and don't do, take action in spite of your worries and prove your inner critic wrong.*

## Message

It's common—normal even—to have moments of doubt, of feeling you're not good enough, and questioning your abilities and worthiness. A little doubt is useful, pushing you to work hard and prepare well. But a complete lack of confidence can keep your life small, and prevent you from achieving all you're capable of. Prevent you from even trying. When anxiety has you in its clutches, you don't go after what you want, push yourself to achieve a goal, confess how you feel to the person you want a relationship with, apply for the job of your dreams or pursue a passion project. But you can change this.

No one is good at everything. Some of the people you admire are terrified to put themselves forward too, because of their own crippling self-doubt. But they do it anyway, and so should you. Stand in your power and express faith in yourself. Self-doubt is the enemy of creativity, progress and joy, and makes it easy to slip into pessimism and despair. It's also a lie, a figment of your imagination, and you have the power to banish it. When you catch yourself saying something nasty, talk back, telling your inner critic it's wrong, and doesn't get to define you. Listen to the voice within you that *does* believe in you, that encourages you to persevere and have faith in yourself. That tells you what's possible, and why you should keep trying. Like a spark that can be nurtured into a wildfire, amplify it until it drowns out the other voice.

Listening to your inner critic is a green light for doubt and second-guessing, and taking action is the best way to silence it. Choose discipline over doubt, and doing it anyway over waiting until you're ready, as it's in the doing that you will become ready and capable. Procrastination is a symptom of self-doubt, because it can paralyse you into inaction. Instead, channel your doubts and use them as fuel to motivate you to try even harder. Undertake your task for its own sake, for the joy of it, and remember your why, focusing on the reasons you started. Then take a deep breath, square your shoulders, place your metaphorical crown on your head — and step forward to claim all the things you so richly deserve.

## Helpful Deities

Call on Ala, the West African earth goddess who is often depicted sitting on a gold throne, to boost your confidence and help you connect with the inner voice that believes in you and understands the importance of your actions. Considered the mother of all things, Ala encourages as well as comforts, while her fellow orisha Oshun, the goddess of love, freedom, abundance and creation, helps instil confidence, independence, strong will and self-esteem in those who work with her, and is considered the maintainer of spiritual balance.

## Affirmations

I am worthy.

I am loved.

I am capable of so much more than I imagine.

I am regal and in control.

I am cool, calm and collected, and eager to step out of my comfort zone.

34. Cut to the Truth

# 34. Cut to the Truth

*Look within to see who you truly are, and realise what is most important to you. Then extend that outwards to everyone you deal with. Being honest can be a revolutionary act, but wield your truth-telling with empathy and kindness.*

## Message

Sometimes the truth is hard to tell, and sometimes it's hard to hear. It can bring you closer to someone and put you on a path to healing, or it can wound deeply. It can be wielded like a sword of justice, cutting away pretence and getting to the heart of the matter, or it can slice through someone's heart and destroy them. Be wary of those who brag about their brutal honesty — often, it's just an excuse to be mean. Because truth is subjective. What's true for you is not necessarily true for anyone else. Few issues are starkly black and white, and people's concept of truth is shaped by their own experiences, beliefs and views of the world.

Your truth can also change over time. Maybe you were devoted to a religion or form of spirituality, until a different path called you. Perhaps you never wanted children, until suddenly you did. You weren't lying before, and you shouldn't lie now — you can only explain what's in your heart, as gently as possible, and allow others the space to react. Try to bear this in mind if a friend or loved one has a change of heart too, and be as understanding and patient as you can.

Be honest. Speak the truth. Seek the truth. Be the truth. Stop hiding who you are, or covering up your self, your beliefs, and your dreams. Showing vulnerability and the truth of who you are is a beautiful gift to offer someone, and an honouring of who you are. Most importantly, be honest with yourself. Acknowledge how you really feel about the situation you face. It's okay to be jealous, angry, frustrated or sad, but denying or repressing your emotions can make you lash out, compromise your morals or keep you stuck. In contrast, understanding and naming what you're feeling can help you work out why you're upset, and the best way to handle it.

Sadly, we live in a post-truth world, surrounded by conspiracy theories, excuses, lies and half-truths. It's more important than ever to check your sources, examine motives and look beneath the surface of the stories you're told. Be discerning in what you pass on to others too, and cautious about who you trust to be telling the truth, and who you trust to hear yours.

## Helpful Deities

Call on Aletheia, the Greek goddess of truth and disclosure, for courage in speaking what is in your heart, and to express your truths clearly and eloquently. The personification of truth, sincerity and 'unconcealment', Aletheia is variously described as a daughter of Zeus and a sculpted creation of Prometheus, the god of fire, who made her to modify human behaviour. You can also work with Veritas, the Roman goddess of truth, who shares many of the same qualities as Aletheia. The Romans worshipped her as they believed truth-telling was one of the most important virtues, and she can be invoked today for the same purpose.

## Affirmations

I will speak my truth.

I have the courage to tell people what I need.

I can be honest, and gentle with my honesty.

I embrace my authentic self.

I weigh up other people's truths carefully.

# 35. It's Time

*Making excuses and avoiding effort might make you happy in the short term, but it will eventually lead to regret, anger and disappointment in yourself. Decide how you want your future to look, then break the procrastination habit and take action now to fulfil your dreams.*

## Message

It's not easy to 'just do it'. Procrastination is often triggered because what you want to do will take effort. It will challenge you, make you uncomfortable and require sacrifice — of your time, of other things you want to do, of the easy stuff that gives you a dopamine hit and seems more fun in the moment. Procrastination is your brain's way of protecting you from the unpleasantness of too much effort. In the same way the brain makes you flee danger, it prompts you to avoid difficult tasks. So you have to override it, and make yourself get to work.

Don't quit on your life or your dreams. Don't put off the things you want to do, or settle for something that doesn't make you happy. Don't let things just happen to you, remaining passive in your own life. It's been said we have 4000 weeks on this planet, if we're lucky. So, if there's something you want to do, do it now. Don't waste another day, another week, another year. Stop saying you'll do it tomorrow. Make the time now. Sit in that hard space and embrace the challenge. Fight for yourself and your dreams.

Procrastination is a habit, so you can break it and choose a better, more productive one instead. Decide to stop procrastinating, then physically take action to reinforce this new proactive you. Recognise that the short-term dopamine hit you'll get from doing something fun will soon be superseded by anxiety and stress from still not having completed your task. If this doesn't help you get moving, use the brain's motivation in reverse. Rather than scrolling aimlessly, getting lost in a new book or binge-watching a series *before* doing what you need to do, offer them as a reward once you've achieved your goal. Focus on how great you'll feel when you've completed your task, instead of the familiar anxiety, stress, dread and depression, and enjoy the sensation of no longer being the major obstacle to your own joy.

What do you need to start doing in order to start doing? Often, the first step is the hardest, so dive in, then use the momentum of your progress to keep up the impetus and remain committed to your goal.

## Helpful Deities

Call on Ganesha, the Hindu god of wisdom and abundance, for help in eliminating all the things that are impeding you—which includes you—from achieving your goals. Known as the remover of obstacles, Ganesha can bless your project and imbue you with wisdom, endurance (like the elephant, whose head he has) and perseverance. The son of Parvati, the benevolent mother goddess, and her husband Shiva, the god of destruction, Ganesha is also a deity of adaptability and beginnings, so he can be invoked before rituals and for any auspicious occasion.

## Affirmations

I can do hard things.

I will make the most of every moment.

I embrace the challenge of achieving my dream.

It's time to make my mark.

I am capable and will complete this project with ease and joy.

36. Feel Your Fire

# 36. Feel Your Fire

*Learning to feel and express anger positively can help
you set boundaries, focus your emotions and instigate
important changes in your life. Just don't let rage rule you.
Acknowledge your anger, channel it in healthy ways to
create positive transformation, then let it go.*

## Message

Anger can be destructive, or a catalyst for transformation.
It's a powerful tool to clear what you no longer need—guilt,
pain, sorrow, the past—so you can rebuild yourself anew,
a phoenix rising from the ashes. It's a fiery, active energy,

challenging you to look within, burn off what drags you down, and awaken the power lying dormant within you. If you channel, direct and calmly express your anger, it can be a force for good, a fiery fuel to drive you forward. A powerful motivator. Justice in action. A revitalisation of your path and purpose.

It can be useful with what you're facing now. Rather than allowing resentment to grow, identify the cause of your rage, and determine if there's anything you can do to change it. If someone's hurting you, let them know, in the hope they'll alter their behaviour. Change your own if that helps, revise your expectations, or offer solutions to solve the problem. If it's something that can't be changed, you'll need to accept it and protect yourself, find a way to avoid the issue, or remove yourself completely from the situation.

For people who grew up with a parent with anger issues or around violence, it can be triggering to have someone mad at them, even if you're calm and don't direct the anger at them. If you've experienced a fury-filled person in the past, it can be challenging to feel anger rise within—you may be scared you'll lose control—but being aware of it means you won't. For it's not anger itself that's bad; it's what you do with it that can be damaging. When upset, some lash out without considering the consequences, unintentionally hurting loved ones or burning bridges they later regret. Others turn their fury inward and punish themselves. Still others swallow their rage, repressing, hiding or denying it completely, so it eats away at them, or finally erupts like a volcano and consumes them — and often those around them too. But you have the power to respond differently. To use it as fuel, rather than allowing it to use you.

Once you've used anger's cleansing power, release it from your mind and body, and embrace the calm that comes after an emotional storm. Then you can rebuild on a stronger, more positive foundation, because anger's energy of creation is just as important as its destructive force, and just as powerful.

# Helpful Deities

Call on Pele, the Hawaiian goddess of transformation, fiery passion and change, who represents the primordial energy of destruction followed by creation, which is the perfect metaphor for how to deal with anger productively and not let it drown you. Tap into Pele's power to focus her fury into action, then switch to the growth and compassion of creation before letting your anger go, so you can rebuild your life and your self in the ways you want to. Associated with volcanoes, fire and creation, Pele will help you transform your anger into action, so your bitterness can melt away and you can release your resentment.

# Affirmations

I embrace the power of my anger as an instigator for change.

I welcome my fury as a positive force, and as motivation to create the life I desire.

I will harness this emotion's energy to take action, then release it once it's spent.

I will learn from my anger, not wallow in it.

When the storm passes, I am at peace.

# 37. Forge Connections

*You deserve people around you who love, respect and care for you, and to honour that by being supportive in turn. Close friendships improve physical and emotional health and overall quality of life. Nurture and nourish your relationships and prioritise reaching out to people, for everybody's sake.*

## Message

In some ways, life has never been easier than it is now, yet many are more miserable and stressed than ever, thanks in part to growing division, isolation and loneliness.

Connections once taken for granted—with work colleagues, friends and family members—may have been challenged, and for some it's been hard, even impossible, to repair them. Everyone craves some human connection, even those who also require time on their own, and loneliness can have serious impacts on mental and physical health. Online connection can be a comfort, but face-to-face time can be even more important, releasing feel-good hormones and building trust and encouragement.

This card is a message to focus on friendships and prioritise personal relationships. Reach out to those you care about. Ask for their support when you need it, and check in with them so you can help in return. Call a friend, organise a visit, start a book club, sign up for a fascinating class, join a theatre troupe or choir, volunteer at a charity you resonate with, or find a support group to help you cope with an issue, and give as much as you receive within it. Find your people and your places, whether it's in your area, online or in another state or even country. You're not alone, and not the only person who feels as you do, struggles with what you're facing, or is enduring the same challenge, illness, obstacle or feeling of despair. Gratefully accept people's support and guidance when it's offered, put yourself out there so others can find you too, and pay it forward by supporting and guiding somebody else.

Emotions are complex and multi-layered, and sometimes you need to look below the surface feeling to what is causing them, triggering them or repressing them. More than just sad, for example, you may be grief-stricken, disappointed, hurt, lonely or in despair. Instead of the catch-all of angry, perhaps you're anxious, contemptuous, jealous or shamed. And are you simply happy, or is it satisfaction, awe, gratitude, excitement, joy or relief? Identifying your emotions helps you understand the full scope of what you're feeling, and work through it in practical, positive ways, resolving your current mood and what's causing it.

## Helpful Deities

Call on Philotes, the Greek goddess of friendship, brotherhood and sisterhood, to help you deepen the bonds with your friends and family members, smooth misunderstandings when they arise, and aid you in staying connected with your loved ones and yourself. The personification of affection and mateship, Philotes was the daughter of Nyx, the primordial Greek goddess of the night. You can also work with Mitra, the Hindu god of the sun, friendship, harmony and integrity, whose name means ally, to help your friendships flourish.

## Affirmations

I value my friendships and work to be a good friend.

I nurture personal connections and place importance on keeping in touch.

I acknowledge my emotions and express my feelings.

I reach out a hand to others who may be sad or lonely.

I deserve to have people in my life who love me.

Making new friends is fun and joyous.

# 38. Keep Going

*Be persistent and persevere, and you will get to your goal eventually. Consistency has magical qualities, so continue onward diligently, not letting setbacks derail you or challenges discourage you from your path. Stay focused on your endpoint and ignore the distraction of shiny new ideas that try to halt your progress.*

## Message

Life is full of stress and angst, darkness and discouragement, but don't let that stop you pursuing your dreams. Keep moving. Make steady progress. It's all you can do, and all you have to do. Go as slow as you need to, pause to breathe when you must. One small movement forward. One moment of love and hope. One CV sent, one page written, one lesson learned or taught. One small action in the direction you want your life to go.

This card is a message to continue. To not give up. It's easy enough to start something when you're filled with the excitement of a bright new idea and inspired by the positive energy it generates. It's far more challenging to keep going when the initial enthusiasm has faded and reality has set in. When you encounter the setbacks that make some people give up. But not you. Persistence is a superpower. It's the drive to keep going when you've realised it's not as simple as you imagined. It's what separates those who are all talk from those who'll turn their determination into results.

There will be challenges, yet if you see them not as blocks to your progress but as signposts to show you a smoother path or different way of thinking, they'll become positive parts of your journey, reinforcing what you're dreaming into being. How you see things, and how well you go with the flow, are choices you make. Switch to a glass-half-full attitude and trust that any seeming obstacle is for a reason. You could dwell on the inconvenience, stubbornly trying to stick to the original plan, or investigate the path that's unfolding, grateful to avoid pitfalls and for all you're learning on this journey.

Whether you believe in fate and destiny or not, make the best of each opportunity offered, forging a 'fate' you're directing every scene of. You have the power to create the life and career and group of loved ones you desire, so hang in there. It will get better. Like grit and determination, persistence is a strength that can be practised and perfected. Keep going. Rise strong. Be the light moving forward in the darkness, illuminating the pathway for others and for yourself. Embrace the challenges and relish the conquering of them, and go after what you want until you succeed.

## Helpful Deities

Call on Demeter, the Greek goddess of determination, to lend you strength and patience, and the ability to find the perseverance that is within you. She never gave up in her search for her daughter Persephone, and her motherly love and endurance can help you continue even when it feels all hope is lost and your metaphorical winter will never end. Demeter was prepared to sacrifice everything—including the world—for what was most important to her, and persisted in the face of lies, denials, cover-ups and difficulties until she achieved her goal and found who she was looking for.

# Affirmations

I shall persist and persevere.

My dreams are worthy of being pursued.

I am grateful for the signs along the way, and follow them with faith and confidence.

This goal is within reach.

I've got this.

# 39. The Ties That Bind

*Being kind doesn't mean being constantly available or always putting others before yourself. Sometimes the kindest thing is to encourage someone to stand on their own two feet and embrace their self-responsibility and inner power. It's time to break the chains of dependence and set some clear boundaries.*

## Message

Are you the one people come to for support, yet you never have the gesture returned when you need someone to care about you? It's time to change your role. It's not your responsibility to fix everyone's problems or be an unpaid counsellor to everyone in your life. Help if and when you can, but know you're not obligated to solve someone's difficulties, or drop everything to be available at a moment's notice, especially if it's a habit that's impacting your own life.

If you always feel drained after spending time with someone, or dread answering the phone because you'll be subjected to a lengthy rant or demand for attention and assistance, strengthen your boundaries. For your own health and wellbeing, stop being constantly available. Don't take on other people's issues at your own expense, or allow their problems to overshadow your own.

It's not healthy for you, and it's not good for others to become dependent on you either, which will happen if you keep helping and making decisions for them. They need to figure things out, take responsibility for their choices, understand their relationships and become independent. Be supportive by all means, but make sure they can recognise their own issues and work out solutions themselves. Just as importantly, focus on balancing the emotional slate, encouraging them to listen to your problems and help you when you need it, so you're not the only one giving.

Check in with your motivation for helping too. It's fine to feel good when you can help others, but becoming too invested in the outcome of other people's issues, or needing to be seen as the saviour, spells trouble for both of you. Having someone be dependent on you for their happiness might be flattering, but it's not sustainable for you or them. And if it's more about you and the endorphin rush you get from their gratitude, it's time to take stock, make changes and loosen the ties that bind you to your role as counsellor and fixer. You don't have to sacrifice all your energy for someone to like you and find you worth hanging out with. Develop the self-esteem to protect and defend your precious time for yourself, and choose friends who care about you as much as you care about them.

## Helpful Deities

Call on Danu, the Celtic mother goddess who is filled with care and compassion, for help in disentangling yourself from the constant needs of others, and releasing your belief that you must sacrifice your own wellbeing to be liked. Associated with wisdom, nature, regeneration and self-love, Danu is the mother of the Tuatha De Danann, and counterpart to the Celtic god Dagda. You can also work with Guanyin, the Buddhist deity of compassion, mercy and relief from suffering, who can guide you in maintaining your independence and setting boundaries while remaining filled with kindness and empathy.

# *Affirmations*

I am worthy of care and attention.

I'm helping out of love, not obligation.

I am only responsible for my own wellbeing.

I replenish my own cup before assisting others.

It's time to cut the ties and ease the dependence.

I empower others by allowing them to find their own solutions.

40. What Matters Most

# 40. What Matters Most

*You are the sum of the things you actually do, not what you dream of doing, so stop waiting for the perfect time to make a change and do something you love today. Finding purpose and meaning will put you in a state of flow and brighten your light.*

## Message

When did you last do something fun? It's easy to get so caught up in work, family and responsibilities that you forget to make time for yourself and the things that bring you joy. If it's been a while since you've had an adventure,

plan one. Indulge your curiosity. Do something unexpected.
Take a risk. Sometimes all you need to reset your life and
reawaken your passion is to step out of your comfort zone
for a moment and gain some perspective.

Pay attention to what you pour all your time and energy
into. Is it what you actually want to dedicate yourself to,
or is it stopping you from being who and what you want
to be? Identify what you're worrying about, and consider
how important it is. Would the world really end if you took
a break, left a task for someone else to finish or said no
to someone's demand on your time — or might it instead
bring you fulfilment, replenish your creative well and make
everything else a little easier to bear?

Pinpoint what's most important to you, and consider why
you haven't been doing it. Then do it, or at least make a
plan to do it. Discover what gives purpose to your life and
puts you into a state of flow, and do the things that make
you feel joyous and alive. Don't wait for a health challenge
or a funeral to give you a wake-up call — spend time *today*
pondering what really matters to you. The dream that
fills your heart with longing, the person you yearn to see
more of, the place you want to visit, the thing you've been
putting off doing until ... *insert excuse here.*

There's never an uninterrupted block of spare time to
nourish your soul — there's only now. Make space in
your life to do what you love, and if you don't know yet,
leap in and figure it out as you go. Don't get to your
deathbed regretting all the things you didn't do. Nothing

is guaranteed, so let go of obligation, even just for a short time, and do something that lights up your heart. You are what you do every day, not what you say you want to do, so if what you're filling your days with isn't who you want to be or part of the life you want to lead, *now* is the time to change.

# Helpful Deities

Call on Bridie, the Celtic maiden goddess of the new moon and new beginnings, and patron of healing, fire and poetry. She brings happiness, inspiration and creativity, as well as the strength to focus on your dreams and light your inner fire. Working with her will help you ignite creative sparks, illuminate the metaphorical darkness, and work through writer's block and other obstacles to your progress. You can also invoke Aengus, the Irish god of love, joy and inspiration, for assistance in finding what makes your heart sing, or Baldur, a Norse god with similar qualities.

# Affirmations

My dreams are important.

I welcome adventure and embrace curiosity.

I follow my bliss to see where it leads.

I have no excuses and no regrets.

I embrace the flow state and will ride its waves.

# 41. Speak Your Truth

*Take care with your words. Don't allow misunderstandings or confusion to blossom. Be brave enough to reveal your inner self to those you are closest to, and consider the courage it takes others to share their true selves too. Honour the gift that it is to show vulnerability and authenticity.*

## Message

Words can be tools of healing and inspiration, or weapons that wound. Your voice is powerful and precious, and your right to use it is a deep part of you. It can be hard to tell someone your truth, but there are times when speaking what's in your heart is so important that you must risk the potential cost. It requires bravery and vulnerability to explain how you feel or reveal part of yourself — and there may be a time when someone offers you the same gift, so receive their opinion or point of view in the spirit in which it's intended, honouring their courage if nothing else, and don't lash out at the messenger.

People can't magically read your mind, so don't assume they'll know how you feel or what you want if you don't share it with them. Everyone acts and reacts from their own experience, so what seems clear to you may not even occur to someone else. Likewise, ask for clarity around their truths, rather than guessing what they mean or attributing motives they don't have.

Speaking your truth is challenging, but necessary for respect and understanding to flourish. Once you name something, you can't ignore it. Labelling an experience or emotion helps you comprehend it and face it. Be aware of how you use your words and who you offer them to. Dedicating all your time to someone just because they demand it, while ignoring the one you care most about because you assume they don't need attention and reassurance, breeds hurt and resentment.

Share your hopes, dreams and problems with loved ones. It's better to be your authentic self than try to hide, and squeeze yourself into someone else's idea of you. Know your limits, and express them — don't leave people to guess. You have no idea how one throwaway comment from you could change someone's life, for good or ill. So speak wisely. Speak well. Speak kindly. Just as you can inspire someone to choose a new path or see the world in a new way, you could crush their spirit too. Equally, your silence can injure someone who needs to know how you feel or craves your support and your witnessing, so don't hide your truth from them, or ignore theirs.

# Helpful Deities

Call on Hermes, the Greek god of science, art, speech, eloquence, writing and boundaries, and messenger of the gods, to spark your courage to always say what you mean, mean what you say, and speak your own truth, even when it's difficult. You can also invoke Nabu, the ancient Mesopotamian god of literacy, wisdom, writing, scribes and the arts, to help you weave your words kindly and with the best of intentions, requesting that he ensure you're not misunderstood.

# Affirmations

I speak my truth.

I am courageous enough to say what I feel and what I mean.

I will ask for clarification when I don't understand what someone has said to me.

I am kind as well as honest.

I honour the truth, even when it hurts.

# 42. Celebrate It All

*To stay inspired, honour the small victories along the path to your objective and celebrate each one. Celebrating yourself and your achievements is an affirmation that will boost your mood and your productivity, helping you face obstacles and keep going, and lighting up the reward centre of your brain.*

## Message

When you're working towards a goal, it's easy to become so focused on the destination that you lose sight of the journey. But you'll miss out on so much if you overlook each phase, from the lessons offered in the frustrating moments to the simple joys and sense of achievement in each stage of progress. So pause. Sit a while. Breathe. Take stock. Instead of focusing only on how far you still have to go, celebrate what you've already accomplished and how far you've already come.

There are so many small victories on the journey to attaining your goal, yet they're often overlooked, not judged significant enough to celebrate. But appreciating each success—no matter its size—and marking it in some way, gives you an emotional boost and helps you keep going. It will remind you why you're working so hard to achieve your dream, and the energy of each small win will encourage you and propel you forward with renewed vigour.

This means more than just stopping to smell the roses. It's cultivating an attitude that allows you to invest your whole journey with importance, and thus your whole life — signalling to your spirit that each small bit of progress is valuable, and firing you up with enthusiasm and passion to continue. Rewarding yourself provides motivation and refocuses your energy. In an era where attention spans are short and long-term goals seem too hard and too far away to bother with, the dopamine hit of many smaller successes will keep you engaged. Mark each win on a calendar, start a journal to keep track, or celebrate with a small gift or reward — be it a thing, an event, or just time to curl up and read. Something meaningful to you, to honour your process and your progress.

Celebrate your seeming failures too. They're an important part, helping refine your goal and what you actually want to achieve, teaching you what doesn't work, developing resilience and determination, and gifting you experience and humility. The journey really is as important as the destination, so allow yourself to enjoy every moment of it — the good and bad, the hard and not-so-hard, the troubles and the triumphs, as well as the person that each step is helping you become. And once you reach your ultimate goal, have a big celebration — then leap into your next adventure and start the pilgrimage towards your next dream.

## Helpful Deities

Call on Lakshmi, the Hindu goddess of success and fortune, for help on your journey, and the wisdom to appreciate both the ups and the downs as you work to attain your goal. Associated with gentleness, abundance, protection and fertility—both literally and of your hopes and dreams— Lakshmi inspires faith in the future and in your success. She can help you visualise the path you will take to get there and guide you in creating a schedule, so you have more time for rest and to do what's important to you.

# *Affirmations*

Each small step towards my goal is valuable.

I appreciate the wins achieved as well as the obstacles in my way.

I love who I am becoming as I work towards my dream.

I honour each part of the journey.

I'm worthy of celebration and self-belief.

# 43. Affirm Your Worth

*Your thoughts are more powerful than you imagine. Big or small, your beliefs have a profound impact on your feelings and actions — even when they're not actually true. Become aware of your self-talk and be kinder to yourself.*

## Message

The words you speak, the thoughts you think and the phrases you write have immense power, which increases manyfold with repetition. Fill your day with positive affirmations, and you'll feel motivated and energetic. Wallow in self-criticism and negative affirmations, and you'll spiral into darkness. Everything you say or think is an affirmation — and it's up to you what you focus on.

Spend a day taking note of everything you say or think — good and bad. Write the positive affirmations on one sheet of paper, the negative on another. Celebrate the positive ones, and read them out again to reinforce them. Congratulate yourself for your commitment to creating a life of joy and success. Then go through the negative ones. It can be unsettling, because most will be so obviously untrue. How many times did you say, "I'm so stupid," when you know that you're not, or "Everyone hates me," which is patently false? Cross these statements out and replace them with true ones that negate them. "I am intelligent." "I am loved and valued."

Next consider the more insidious ones. Are you affirming statements like "there's just no point", or "I have no chance of getting that", or "bad things always happen to me"? These statements might not be blatant lies, but repeating them can add to your despair, make you want to give up before you even start, and turn them into self-fulfilling prophecies. These ones can be harder to address and require more vigilance than the wildly untrue ones, so remind yourself often that you'll no longer say them.

Sometimes, however, a negative affirmation is true, which can be a wonderful opportunity for growth. Look at your negative list. Is it time to face something that's holding you back, and finally do something about it? If you're indecisive and it bothers you, concentrate on making decisions. If you always choose the wrong partner or friend, take things slower when you meet people and be more discerning. If you don't exercise but want to be healthier and fitter, start small and work your way up. Once you understand everything is an affirmation—you are affirming life is wonderful, or terrible—you can take charge of your thoughts and create the present and the future you want.

# Helpful Deities

Call on Amaterasu, the Shinto sun goddess whose name means 'shining in heaven', for assistance in building your self-esteem and affirming your worth. Let Amaterasu help you see beneath the walls you've put up and into your beautiful heart, so you can understand and recognise your strength, value and magic. Alongside her siblings, Amaterasu is thought to have created Japan and painted its beautiful landscape into being, and she gifted a sacred mirror to her descendants, so they could see themselves shining — a metaphorical gift you can look into in order to see your own light too.

# Affirmations

Choose the affirmation you really need to work on, and incorporate it into your day somehow — write it down, stick it on a mirror or in your phone, pop it under your pillow, make it into art, discuss it with a friend, say it every hour, or post it on social media and begin a discussion about it. Once you have a handle on this one, add new affirmations, either individually for deeper work, or alternate a few.

44. Hold On to Hope

# 44. Hold On to Hope

*To bring more hope, joy, love and light into your life, embody these qualities and behave as though you are already abundant with them. Find one little spark of light and nurture it, fanning it into a blazing flame of inspiration, and lighting the way forward for yourself and others.*

## Message

It can be hard to keep your faith in yourself and the world, but holding on to hope is essential. It gives you a reason to get up each day, and to keep aiming for your goals even when it feels too hard. Hope is courage, self-belief and confidence. It's backing yourself and having certainty that you'll succeed, despite naysayers. Knowing you'll find a way forward through persistence and sheer grit. And the more you believe, the more you'll succeed, giving you more hope and thus more belief, in a wonderful cycle of realistic optimism and enthusiasm.

Some people consider hope a weakness, but it can be your greatest strength. It's the force that will keep you moving through sadness and frustration. It's not blind optimism or toxic positivity, denying the reality of a situation or the size of an obstacle. It's not living in a fantasy land. Hope is the part of you that accepts the enormity of the task and is convinced you'll find a way through, even if you can't see it yet.

If you're struggling to find hope, look for acts of kindness and focus on those. In a crisis, search for the helpers, taking comfort from their existence. Surround yourself with beauty and nature, and those who are positive, encouraging and supportive. Reach out to friends and loved ones, and allow them to boost your mood, inspire you and remind you of all you're capable of. Be each other's light and cheer each other on.

Recall previous successes and how you achieved them, and reflect on past moments of joy and how you embodied them physically. You've felt before the hope you seek now, and it will return. Be gentle with yourself if you're struggling. Keep looking for the glimmer of light within. It's always there, even if it's only the tiniest flicker you must carefully nurture into a flame. There's always something to celebrate and be grateful for. It doesn't always have to be something for you. Perhaps bringing joy to someone else is enough for the moment, or a new way for you to grow will provide hope. You *can* find happiness in the darkest of times if you search for that tiny spark — or if you *become* the light, a beacon of hope for yourself and others and an inspiration to all.

# Helpful Deities

Call on Elpis, the Greek goddess of hope, whose name means hope, faith, expectation, trust and confidence. When Pandora opened the jar Zeus had entrusted her with, unleashing sickness, fear, strife and pain on the world, Elpis, the last spirit in the jar, decided to stay, to provide hope to humanity. She's depicted as a young woman holding flowers in her arms, and sometimes the cornucopia or horn of plenty to imply abundance, and was considered at the time the only good deity remaining among humankind. You can also work with Elpis' counterpart, the Roman nature goddess Spes, who was considered the personification of hope for a successful harvest and an abundance of offspring, and hope, luck and good fortune in life and love.

# *Affirmations*

I can do this.

There is light in every darkness, and I will find it.

I am filled with hope, which spills out from me in ever-growing circles.

I embody light and shine it outwards.

I gratefully accept the support and encouragement of others, and offer it in turn.

# About the Author

Serene Conneeley is an Australian writer, witch and healer with a fascination for history, travel, ritual and the myth and magic of ancient places and cultures. She's written for magazines about news, travel, health, spirituality, entertainment, and social and environmental issues, written and edited teen and kids publications, and contributed to books on witchcraft, history, psychic development and personal transformation.

She is the author of six non-fiction titles—*Witchy Magic*, *Mermaid Magic* and *Faery Magic* with Lucy Cavendish, and *Seven Sacred Sites*, *A Magical Journey* and *Sacred Journey*—as well as **Practical Magic: An Oracle for Everyday Enchantment**. Her novels include the *Into the Mists* and *Into the Storm* trilogies and several original faery tales, including *The Swan Maiden*, *The Wattle Wife* and *The Snow Queen's Daughter*.

Serene is a member of the Australian Fairy Tale Society and has studied magical and medicinal herbalism, bereavement counselling, bibliotherapy, Reconnective Healing®, Reiki and other healing modalities, plus politics and journalism. She loves reading books, drinking tea, working out, being in nature, and celebrating the energy of the moon and the magic of the earth. Her pagan heart blossomed as she climbed mountains, danced in stone circles, swam with dolphins, crawled into ancient burial mounds, stood in the shadow of the pyramids and did rituals with shamans and priestesses on her travels, and she's also, perhaps more importantly, learned the magic of finding true happiness and peace at home.

Learn more about Serene at *sereneconneeley.com*

# About the Artist

A self-taught illustrator with a degree in art history, Cecilia G.F. uses her knowledge of symbology and art theory to enrich her works with meaning. She draws inspiration from many sources, including music, books, video games and mythology.

Cecilia's artwork features in the Blue Angel Publishing titles *The Queen Mab Oracle* (authored by Tess Whitehurst) and *The Goddess Within Oracle* and *Divine Masculine Healing Oracle* (both by Christabel Jessica).

Cecilia has collaborated with publishers such as Alethé, Supersonic, Nocturna, Kakao Books and Munyx and has worked with clients from all over the world. Some of her best-known cover images are *Clorofilia* by Cristina Jurado (for which she won the Ignotus Award in 2018), *La Compañía Amable* by Rocío Vega, *Sistemas Críticos* by Martha Wells and *El Clan Sin Nombre* by África Vázquez Beltrán.

Discover more of Cecilia's works by connecting with ThanatosofNicte on Twitter, Instagram and Twitch, or Ceciliagf on ArtStation.

*NOTES:*

# NOTES:

# NOTES:

*NOTES:*

# Bonestone & Earthflesh Tarot

*Avalon Cameron*
*Artwork by Ana Tourian*

This evocative tarot deck weaves together myth, magic, and ancestral wisdom to guide you through sacred landscapes and timeless archetypes. A powerful new edition of the beloved original, it invites mystics and seekers to remember, explore, and connect with the primal forces that shape the inner and outer worlds.

Cauldron Sisters
THREE OF CUPS

Young Merlin the Apprentice
PAGE OF SWORDS

The Shadow Emissary
SEVEN OF SWORDS

79 cards + 384-page colour guidebook.  ISBN:  978-1-922574-47-3

# Soul Reflections Tarot

*Sunshine Connelly*
*Artwork by Ana Novaes*

Designed to support deep personal growth through the practice of Soul Mirroring. This deck blends traditional tarot structure with intuitive insight and expressive, symbolic artwork — inviting you to explore your inner world, release what no longer serves you, and align with your highest potential.

Two of Cups

III. The Empress

0. The Fool

78 cards + 288-page colour guidebook. ISBN: 978-1-922574-40-4

Also available from Blue Angel Publishing

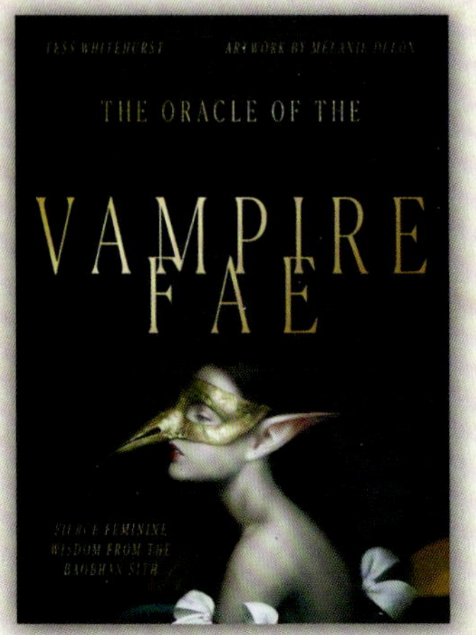

## The Oracle of the Vampire Fae

*Tess Whitehurst*
*Artwork by Mélanie Delon*

Channel the ancient wisdom of the enigmatic Scottish vampire fae — ethereal shapeshifters who appear as radiant women, elusive wolves, and majestic ravens. These master alchemists transform stagnant energy and outdated beliefs into radiant strength and beauty.

52 cards + 128-page colour guidebook.  ISBN:  978-1-922574-49-7

# The Wild Witch Oracle

*Tess Whitehurst*
*Artwork by Tammy Wampler*

Featuring 44 bold heroines, *The Wild Witch Oracle* delivers messages that enliven your courage to create a life that's truly authentic. From astrological goddesses to nature sprites, faerie queens to historical monarchs, the supernatural and the human collide, awakening your innate divine powers.

44 cards + 160-page colour guidebook.  ISBN:  978-1-922574-39-8

PUBLISHING

For more information on this or
any other Blue Angel Publishing
release, please visit our website at:

*www.blueangelonline.com*